ELIZABETH I

In memory of my late mother;
Breda Linehan (1956-2019) who always encouraged my love of
reading & the past

This is book dedicated to the many women in history
Who have been forgotten through time;
Although you were not queens
You too faced many of the trials highlighted in this book.

To Ophelia my little shadow

ELIZABETH I

THE MAKING OF A QUEEN

LAURA BRENNAN

PEN & SWORD
HISTORY

AN IMPRINT OF PEN & SWORD BOOKS LTD.
YORKSHIRE – PHILADELPHIA

First published in Great Britain in 2020 by
PEN AND SWORD HISTORY
An imprint of
Pen & Sword Books Ltd
Yorkshire – Philadelphia

ISBN 978 1 52671 457 2

A CIP catalogue record for this book is available from the British Library.

Typeset in Times New Roman 11.5/14 by
Aura Technology and Software Services, India.
Printed and bound in the UK by TJ International.

Pen & Sword Books Limited incorporates the imprints of Atlas, Archaeology,
Aviation, Discovery, Family History, Fiction, History, Maritime, Military, Military
Classics, Politics, Select, Transport, True Crime, Air World, Frontline Publishing,
Leo Cooper, Remember When, Seaforth Publishing, The Praetorian Press,
Wharncliffe Local History, Wharncliffe Transport, Wharncliffe True Crime and
White Owl.

For a complete list of Pen & Sword titles please contact
PEN & SWORD BOOKS LIMITED
47 Church Street, Barnsley, South Yorkshire, S70 2AS, England
E-mail: enquiries@pen-and-sword.co.uk
Website: www.pen-and-sword.co.uk

Or

PEN AND SWORD BOOKS
1950 Lawrence Rd, Havertown, PA 19083, USA
E-mail: Uspen-and-sword@casematepublishers.com
Website: www.penandswordbooks.com

Contents

Acknowledgements

Innocently and probably somewhat naively, I thought that writing a second book would mean that I found the whole process easier than the first time around. How wrong I was; which is why I need to take this opportunity to say a big thank you to the people who have helped me to keep going and cheered me on through this whole process.

Once again, thanks go to Jon Wright and Laura Hirst at Pen & Sword for your constant patience. Thanks also goes to my agent Kate Bohdanowicz for making this possible, and to Lucy Benyon for her thorough and sensitive editing of this book. Lastly, thanks must go to the great staff at the British Library, especially within the humanities reading room, for their patience and help in finding primary sources.

Special thanks go to my brother Mark Linehan, who showed total faith in this project and never doubted my abilities even when I did; supplying me with beer and money when required. To my uncle, Paul Brennan for lunches, gin and chocolate - all total necessities when finishing a draft. To Ruth, Chris and Babs thank you for always being there - I need to take a day trip to the seaside very soon! To Julia Hopkins, thank you for the pep talks from New Zealand, for being a great sounding board, and for pictures of Lottie. To Haley Foster, thank you for your encouragement and kind words. And to Rob Leadbeater, we must have drinks to celebrate in London very soon.

Honourable mention needs to go towards John Broad, my BA Hons dissertation supervisor at London Metropolitan University as he pointed me in the direction of many of the books and sources used in this work. It was him who liked to tell me to edit said dissertation as I was 'not writing a book.' This meant that I always had that extra knowledge and words in my head, wanting to be used, and it was this that eventually made this book possible.

Lastly, thanks go to everyone who has brought this book as well as the first one. You've not only used your valuable time to read my words, but you've also spent hard-earned cash to purchase them. Your support and kind words mean a lot so thank you.

Introduction

There have been hundreds, if not thousands of historical biographies written about England's greatest queen, Elizabeth I. This work is not supposed to be a full blow by blow biography, with details on every single event in Elizabeth's life or reign, it is instead a selection of events that I feel after years of reading about Elizabeth, the period and the social and political environments of the time, help to demonstrate who Elizabeth was and why she acted and made the choices she made both as a very public queen and as a private woman. This book is essentially the undergraduate dissertation I wanted to write for my BA but was told it was far too broad a topic. My dissertation ended up looking at the relationship between Mary Queen of Scots and Elizabeth - a subject which is, almost fifteen years later, very much en vogue with new books and movies coming out on the subject all the time.

Upon starting this work, it felt natural to split the book into two; looking first at Elizabeth's life before and then life after becoming the last Tudor monarch. Each chapter aims to give the historical narrative as well as summing up how I feel the topic affected her decisions and life and why she acted as she did both personally and publicly. This selection of events, spanning the life time of Elizabeth Tudor (1533-1603), are what I considered to be the key to shaping Elizabeth, but they are of course subjective and not everyone will agree with these choices but difference is good as it starts debate and encourages closer examination by the reader.

Included within this work are events that took place outside of England, namely the assassination of William 'The Silent' of Orange, the St Bartholomew's Day massacre as well as a brief look at the reign of Mary Queen of Scots prior to her abdication and exile and imprisonment in England. Both the assassination of William of Orange and the St Bartholomew's day massacre help give context to the plight of Protestants in Europe during Elizabeth's lifetime and an idea of the post-reformation religious struggles in both Europe and England during her reign.

I included the sections dealing with Mary's disastrous return to Scotland to give context in two ways: firstly, to see how and why she ended up crossing the border and seeking help from Elizabeth and also, to give a contrasting depiction of two very different styles of queenship. These two women never met in life and both achieved different aims, one ruled strongly with her head, the other with her heart and passion. Although Mary personally lost the battle, she would ultimately win through the succession of her son James I of England.

The second part of the book looks at Elizabeth the queen, politician and woman, and it attempts to explain why and what may have influenced her decisions and how her past affected the choices she made until her death in 1603. I hope by the end of the book you will get a picture of why I feel Elizabeth ruled as she did during her reign - which is also considered to be a golden age of English monarchy.

Many of the topics covered in these chapters have entire books dedicated to just them; therefore, limited by the confines of the theme and aims of this work, I hope to give you, the reader, a starting point to seek further reading for the events and people mentioned if you want to know more.

Primary sources have been used to create a more authentic story through contemporary witnesses' recorded words in letters and papers found in state documents. These sources allowed me to use the research skills that I had developed as a history student. Quotations from primary sources as well as extracts from English translations of early bibles have been left in Tudor English with Tudor spelling for authenticity unless they were published in a more modern format within the state papers that they were found in.

I have read a wide range of secondary sources (both for this venture and for pleasure), and it is with this knowledge and my take on this period of history that this book has been crafted. I have not knowingly duplicated work or material and I have referred to secondary sources directly.

I have kept names spelt in their native language through personal preference, Mary Queen of Scots has been anglicised to Mary not Maire as she was born in Scotland and returned to Scotland and escaped to

England. I use the spelling Stuart in reference to the Scottish royal house throughout the work for uniformity and consistency. When it comes to the spelling of Henry VIII's wives named Katherine, I use Katherine of Aragon with a K in the anglicised form as she became an English queen instead of using her native Spanish Catrine. For Catherine Howard, I used C to distinguish her from the other two queen consorts who shared her first name, and lastly, I also used K for Katherine Parr as she signed her name Kathryn. There have been variations of spelling for some of the other key people and places in this biography. My aim has been to choose one and to remain consistent throughout. For example, I use the spelling Forthinghay not Forthingay, Amyas Paulet not Poulett, and used Holyroodhouse rather than Holyrood or Holyrood Palace as there are variations of these spellings and titles in both primary and secondary sources. Any discrepancy in this is my fault.

Elizabeth was an effective public relations manager and she used art and rhetoric to portray the image she wanted to convey to her subjects and to history itself. In doing this, she really was her father's daughter. Hopefully, this work will bring context and personality to that image of the 'Virgin Queen' that she fought so hard to preserve until her death in March 1603.

As a modern woman living in the twenty-first century, it is hard to forget that Elizabeth really was breaking the mould as a woman in power during the sixteenth century. She also brought the Tudor age to a conclusion, leaving this troubled dynasty on a high, as well as ending separate monarchies for England and Scotland. This period of English history can be seen as an historical bridge, connecting the history of the medieval ages to the commencement of more enlightened times and the dawn of modernity.

PART 1

ELIZABETH THE PRINCESS

Much suspected by me,
Nothing proved can be

(Reputedly carved into a window by
Lady Elizabeth while held at Woodstock Manor)

1533: The Birth of a Princess

The birth of the royal baby was a day that the whole English court had been waiting for. The king, Henry VIII, was eager to meet his new heir, as he waited impatiently for his wife to give birth in the now lost Greenwich Palace on the bank of the River Thames.

Henry had waited, wished and wanted to make this day happen so badly, that he had not only risked his own immortal soul but the stability of his nation by separating the English church from the dominance and rule of the Holy See and the papacy. The reason Henry had taken this spiritual risk was in order to divorce his first wife and queen, Katherine of Aragon, so that he could marry the younger, and hopefully more fertile, Anne Boleyn. Henry had caused all this disruption in the hope that Anne could give him a much-needed son, but Anne gave him a baby daughter.

Henry had been certain that this royal child would be a much longed for a son. This had been encouraged further by the royal astrologer and even by the queen herself as both had confidently announced that the child was male and destined to be a great king. They may have been wrong about the gender but they were correct about the child's future as Elizabeth did go on, despite the odds, to become a great queen.

Evidence of this unwavering certainty in the gender of the royal child can be found in the correspondence of the Spanish ambassador, Eustace Chapuys. He said the following of Henry; 'believing in the report of his physicians and astrologers that his Lady will certainly give him a male heir [he] has made up his mind to solemnize the event with a pageant and tournament' *(Calendar of State Papers Spain Vol 4 Part 2)*.

Fate, however, had other ideas and at 3.00 pm on Sunday, 7 September, the queen gave birth to a baby girl. Poor Henry had risked so much and was rewarded with the birth of a Princess. Chapuys, who had been Queen Katherine's ambassador, and who was one of the few allies she still had in England, disclosed his personal delight at the fact the baby had been in fact a daughter rather than a son by saying, 'delivered of a girl, to the great disappointment and sorrow of the king, o the Lady herself and of others of her party and to the great shame of physicians, astrologers, wizards and witches, all of whom affirmed it would be a boy.' *(Calendar of State Papers Spain Vol 4 Part 2)*.

The disappointment of the child's gender meant that the planned celebrations, consisting of a jousting tournament and a pageant, were cancelled as such expense was not deemed worthy of a baby girl. Henry had been so convinced of a boy that he had not even thought of a name for his daughter as he had been too busy trying to decide if this heir should be called Edward or Henry. So, with little thought, he named the child after his mother and she was christened Elizabeth three days after her birth, at the church of the Observant Friars in Greenwich. Due to her royal status, Princess Elizabeth was welcomed into the new Church of England by the Bishop of London, John Stokesley and the Archbishop of Canterbury, Thomas Cramner, was given the honour of standing as the little princess's godfather. Princess Elizabeth's godmothers were the Duchess of Norfolk and Marchioness of Dorset.

Anne assumed that following on from her daughter's birth, she would go on to produce a whole host of healthy males for Henry, but there is only evidence of one other pregnancy, which apparently ended in the late miscarriage of a son in January 1535, just over a year before her execution.

1536: The Execution of Anne Boleyn

The rise and fall of Anne Boleyn created one of the most notorious female figures in English history. Henry and Anne's conduct significantly shaped the religious and political landscape of the United Kingdom and its influence can still be felt to this day.

In many ways, Anne and Henry's story can be seen as one of the most romantic tales in history, certainly it looks that way on the surface. The unhappy king falls in 'love' with a young noblewoman just back from the French royal court. Henry had carnally known Anne's sister, Mary, and hoped to get to know Anne just as intimately. The young noblewoman however was not prepared to be used by either her power-hungry father or the king in the same way that her sister had been. Anne used her sexual allure to make Henry do more than desire her body but also to fall in love with her. Once she had him totally besotted with her, Anne manipulated Henry in to finding a way to make her his queen, even though he was already married.

In his pursuit to end his marriage to his long-suffering first wife, Katherine of Aragon, Henry ended up causing an ecclesiastical rift with the Catholic Church. This subsequently triggered the English Reformation and the resulting reforms that would serve Henry's personal agenda to be free of an infertile wife. Subsequently, he had created an English church that became known as the Anglican Church.

Anne had arrived at Henry's court in 1522 and it took her eleven years to get what she wanted and to become Queen of England. The fairytale would not last, and within three years, Anne would become the first English queen to be executed. Not even Henry VIII could execute his wife without following proper legal procedures or without having a legal reason to do so. The Tudor royal court was a hotbed of fractions, alliances and petty politics within the elite classes. All the noble families would plot, plan and manipulate to gain favour and power and to have closer access to the king. Whoever happened to be the monarch's favourite would automatically attract rivals and enemies within the court. Henry turned to Cardinal Wolsey's protégée, a lawyer named Thomas Cromwell, in order to help him find a solution to getting rid of his now unwanted and troublesome second wife. Cromwell manipulated the court cliques and petty alliances to find a way to discredit Anne through her enemies and to 'legally' remove her from the royal marriage; just as men before him had manipulated church law to place Anne upon the throne.

Thomas Cromwell was able to gather enough evidence and witnesses to bring the charges of adultery against Anne. For a queen to commit adultery was seen as high treason. In addition to this charge, she was also accused of witchcraft and incest. Although Anne was charged with adultery, incest and high treason; her biggest crime really was her failure to give Henry his much desired Tudor male heir. On 2 May 1536, Anne's arrest warrant was actioned. At 5.00 pm, she was taken by barge from Greenwich Palace along the River Thames to her final home, the Tower of London. Her goalers for this fateful journey were Cromwell; Anne's uncle, the Duke of Norfolk; the Lord Chancellor, Sir Thomas Audley and finally the Constable of the Tower of London, William Kingston. As they approached the infamous Tower of London, Anne became agitated and distraught. Poor Anne spent her brief residency within The Tower in the very chambers she had used prior to her coronation less than three years before. She could have a small household with her, but the servants had to be selected by Cromwell.

Cromwell could not bring about Anne's demise without incriminating others and in all, seven men were arrested and charged with having sexual relations with the Queen of England. These men were Henry Norris, William Bereton, groom of the king's privy chamber, Sir Francis Weston, Mark Smeaton, a court musician, and her own brother, George Boleyn whose full title was Lord Rochford, and he too was also charged with incest as well as high treason. The sixth and seventh men to be arrested were the poet, Sir Thomas Wyatt and Sir Richard Page. They too were arrested and accused of adultery with the queen. However, unlike the other men, both Page and Wyatt were acquitted of all charges made against them. These men were tried on 12 May in Westminster Hall, and apart from Smeaton, they all denied their guilt. The court ruled against them and they were all found guilty of high treason and were sentenced to a traitor's death.

Anne and her brother George were tried three days later for their charges of adultery, high treason and incest. It is said that throughout her trial Anne denied all charges brought against her, and despite the graveness of the situation, she remained calm and dignified throughout the hearing, giving the court plausible and innocent reasons for each of the times she was said to have committed these crimes. To hold such nerve during a time of extreme fear and distress is testament to Anne's courage. The trial however was merely a procedure, and the outcome was always going to fall in Henry's favour. It was her own uncle, the Duke of Norfolk, who decreed the verdict of guilty and subsequently passed her sentence of death by burning or beheading at the king's pleasure.

On 17 May, Francis Weston, William Brereton and Henry Norris were brought to the designated place of execution upon Tower Hill. As gentlemen they were given the privilege of being beheaded rather than being hung, drawn and quartered for their role in the fall of the Queen Anne. On the same day, Anne's brother George joined these men upon the scaffold, and he too lost his head for his supposed role in his sister's fall from power. Despite being of low birth, Mark Smeaton, who was the only one who confessed his guilt, was also beheaded rather than having to suffer the drawn out and cruel traitor's death.

On 14 May, Cranmer declared that the marriage between Anne and King Henry had never been valid and that consequently it was now null and void in the eyes of the law and the Anglican communion. As her marriage had been voided ahead of her execution, Anne held hope of a last-minute reprieve from the king. Although he intended to carry out the sentence, Henry decided to show Anne the mercy of beheading her rather than having her burnt alive at the stake. He also insured that her death would be swift and performed by a master executioner from France, where beheadings were carried out using a sharp sword rather than an axe. Initially, Anne's death was due to coincide with that of her alleged lovers on 17 May, however the master executioner from France was delayed on his journey granting Anne two extra days.

On the morning of the 19 May, within the curtained walls of The Tower and away from the prying eyes of London, Anne Boleyn, who had managed to rise to become the Queen of England, was led towards a scaffold erected on Tower Green for the purpose of her death. Until the end, Anne put on a show of calm dignity. She crossed The Tower precincts dressed demurely in a sombre grey damascus gown, lined with ermine fur and a red petticoat. Once on the scaffold, Anne made her final speech to the small crowd gathered to watch her die.

'Good Christian People, I am come hither to die, for according to the law and by the law I am judged to die and therefore I will speak nothing against it. I am come hither to accuse no man, nor speak anything of that, whereof I am accused and condemned to die but I pray God save the king and send him long to reign over you, for a gentler nor a more merciful prince was there never: and to me he was ever good, a gentle sovereign Lord. And if any person will meddle of my cause, I require them to judge best. and thus I take my leave of the world and of you all, and I heartily desire you all to pray for me. O Lord have mercy on me, to god I commend my soul.' *(Hall's Chronicle)*

Unlike beheading by axe, no block is required with a master swordsman, Anne knelt down, and her ermine-lined gown was removed. The last service her ladies performed was tying a blindfold over her eyes. The executioner, well-practised in his gruesome art, distracted her with a noise and with one deadly accurate swing of his sword detached her head from her body. Her ladies gathered her remains into a makeshift coffin, that had once held arrows. The late queen's body was then laid to rest within the Tower's chapel of St Peter ad Vincular.

Even today, historians are divided over the charges of adultery against Anne. In my opinion, they were probably groundless, although after her failed attempts to provide Henry with a male heir, there is an argument that she might have tried to procreate with her brother George in an act of absolute desperation, but there is no proof either way.

Elizabeth was four months shy of her third birthday at the time of her mother's death and was obviously far too young to understand the politics surrounding her execution. It is said that when Elizabeth's ring of state was removed after her death in March 1603, the jewel had a secret compartment which had a small painting of her mother.

Anne Boleyn paid a very high price for her inability to give Henry a son. Later on when Elizabeth was a young woman and then after she became queen in her own right, she seems to have taken on board the risks and lessons from her mother's story and was able to successfully avoid ruin by not allowing herself to be controlled by men or suffering an untimely death, despite finding herself in several dangerous predicaments. In many ways, Elizabeth was Anne's greatest triumph and not Henry's as despite the odds, Elizabeth would become queen and would be the most successful monarch of his three children.

1537: The Birth of Prince Edward

The main reason why King Henry VIII became so obsessed with his lack of male heirs and the fertility of his wives, can be traced back to how he himself became king. If fate had been different, Henry would have had a career within the Catholic Church, quite an irony considering it was Henry that triggered the English reformation during his reign. Henry had not been the eldest son and male heir of Henry VII; he had been the royal Tudor spare. Henry's older brother, Prince Arthur, had unexpectedly died on 2 April 1502, leaving the throne and the future of the Tudor royal house to the fate of his younger brother, Henry. He also left a young Spanish widow. It turned out, it was still Katherine of Aragon's fate to become the Queen of England, as she remarried and became Henry VIII's first wife.

Another reason why it was important for Henry to have a legitimate male heir was because the royal House of Tudor was still relatively new and was not as politically secure or established within its status as the ruling royal house of England. This is partly due to the way that the Tudors had claimed the English throne, at the climax of the bitter civil war between the houses of York and Lancaster that is better known as the War of the Roses. Henry's parents married in order to regain political stability and bring the two conflicted sides together; Henry Tudor came from the House of Lancaster and Elizabeth came from the House of York. In order to keep the royal house of Tudor on the hard won English throne, Henry VIII knew he needed to produce male heirs. During the sixteenth century, it was unknown for a princess to be an heir, let alone to inherit the throne and rule in her own right. By 1537, Henry had failed to father any legitimate male heirs. It was not from lack of trying, having divorced his first wife and beheaded his second, he had still only produced two princesses and one acknowledged but illegitimate son, Henry Fitzroy. Fitzroy was fathered with Henry's mistress Elizabeth Blount.

However due to his illegitimate status, Fitzroy would not to be eligible to inherit the throne upon his father's death.

Once Henry was free to re-marry, he did so with much haste. Time was of the essence, as the King of England, if rumours were to be believed, was no longer the once virile young man he had been when he had ascended to the throne. He was no longer the handsome or charming prince he had been in his youth either. Instead Henry had morphed into a stout 45-year-old man who was prone to bouts of ill temper and anger, and yet this temperamental king still required a male heir.

As Thomas Cromwell plotted to bring down Anne, Henry was already moving on emotionally, and he had set his sights on one of his wife's ladies-in-waiting, Lady Jane Seymour. There is no denying that Anne had been passionate, exciting, reformist, dark, mysterious and in many ways, a modern woman, living before her time during the sixteenth century. However, Henry's third choice of wife, Jane, was everything that Anne had not been; she was meek, mild, kind, compassionate, obedient and still a Catholic.

Henry and Jane were officially betrothed the day after Anne was executed upon Tower Green and were subsequently married ten days later on 30 May at Whitehall Palace in London's Westminster. It was a private ceremony, officiated by Bishop Gardiner. The rest of the country was informed of the identity of its new queen consort on 4 June. The public's opinion of Jane was much more favourable than it had been of Anne.

Although Jane was proclaimed queen, she never had an official coronation. The official reason for this was that London was not safe enough during the summer of 1536 due to an epidemic of bubonic plague, which was a regular occurrence during the sixteenth century. However, with the benefit of hindsight, and a slightly cynical twenty-first century historical point of view, it could be suggested that Jane's lack of coronation could well have been a decision made by a frustrated Henry. Was he holding out on crowning her officially until she had done her royal duty and had given him his much needed male Tudor heir?

Henry's new queen did her royal duty in January 1537 when she conceived a child. Jane was 28 when she entered her confinement. The peak child-bearing age in Tudor times was between 20 and 25 and Jane would have been considered an older mother by sixteenth century standards. By all accounts, the royal gestation was said to have run relatively smoothly, and the new queen was said to have taken a particular fancy to quails during her pregnancy. In an attempt to ensure that he finally got his male heir, Henry is said to have ordered the queen her favourite poultry craving from continental mainland Europe.

As per tradition of the day, Jane entered her confinement at the royal palace of Hampton Court on the 16 September ahead of her estimated October delivery date. She started to feel labour pains on 9 October less than a month after going into her laying-in period. She eventually gave birth to Prince Edward during the early hours of the morning of 12 October after three long days of labour. Unfortunately, Jane Seymour was never to leave her birthing chamber. Three days after she had given birth, the queen developed a dangerous fever. As a precautionary measure, she was given the Catholic last rites on the 17 October. The queen fought for her life for a further week before finally dying of childbirth complications on 24 October 1537. The birth of a much wanted and desired male Tudor heir should have been a joyous time for Henry but instead he had been issued with a bittersweet blow by the hand of fate.

The consequences of the birth of Edward and the death of Jane Seymour are twofold for the infant Elizabeth. The arrival of her little half-brother Edward should have meant that Elizabeth wouldn't inherit the throne as Edward should have gone on to have his own heirs to carry on the lineage of the house of Tudor after him. This in turn meant that the young Elizabeth would have been seen as a political and diplomatic tool to be used to strengthen England's ties within Europe. Even though she had been proclaimed illegitimate, she was still the acknowledged daughter of the English King, Henry VIII.

The death of her first stepmother Jane also meant that Elizabeth lost a potential future ally. During her short time as queen, Jane had shown Elizabeth's half-sister Mary great kindness. The reason for this compassion may have been that Jane had disliked what Henry had done to Mary's mother, Katherine of Aragon. It also could have been because both Jane and Mary shared the same Catholic faith (although Jane had practised her religion privately within the Anglican court). Her feeling may also be explained due to their relative closeness in age: both were highborn women, Mary was 21-years-old at the time of Jane's death, and she may have wanted help to settle Mary with the best possible future. Jane had been used by her father for political power gain within Henry's court and she may have hoped to help Mary. Therefore, it is highly likely that Jane may have shown a similar level of care and compassion and towards Henry's younger daughter, Elizabeth once she was older.

Although still too young to have understood much at this time, Elizabeth would have learnt about Jane as she grew up at court. She must have understood the secret to Jane's success was her obedience, something that Elizabeth mimicked during her sister Mary's reign. Although she was a Protestant, she put on a show of obeying her sister and being meek. This would ensure that she stayed alive and was able to go on to become Mary's heir.

1540: The Second & Third Stepmothers of Lady Elizabeth

After the birth of Prince Edward, Henry VIII finally had his legitimate male heir within the Tudor royal nursery. But little Prince Edward had come at a high cost as his mother, Jane, had died in the process. However, with a new Tudor prince, this meant that the king's previous urgency to find a new wife, was not as urgent as before. Yet Thomas Cromwell, Henry's 'fix it' man was given the difficult task of finding the king a fourth wife. After divorcing long-suffering Katherine, beheading Anne and witnessing Jane die in childbirth, Henry's reputation as a husband was hardly appealing and there was not a long line of eligible single ladies lining up for the position of queen at home or in Europe. The purposes of royal marriages were usually to seal political alliances and Katherine of Aragon, Henry's first wife, had been matched with his brother Arthur for such a purpose. But post-reformation England had less options of potential Protestant princess matches, making Cromwell's task even harder.

One of the few Protestant outlets open to Cromwell was Germany. In 1537, Germany was not a united country but a collective of states ruled by various powerful families, overseen by the Holy Roman Emperor, Charles V. This early Germanic territory was also divided by religious conviction. The reform movement had started within the German city of Wittenberg by the Friar Martin Luther, yet there were still provinces that were, and remain today, as Catholic as France or Spain.

The city of Düsseldorf located within the Rhineland area of the German territory was not a predominantly Protestant city, but Duke Johann of Cleves had dismissed papal authority within his territory in a similar way as Henry VIII had done in England and the duke had two daughters; Sibylle and Anne. Sibylle of Cleves had been married off to the Elector of Saxony, who was the leader of the Schmalkaldic League - which was a Protestant, anti-Catholic alliance between Protestant settlements that found themselves under the rule of the Holy Roman Empire. By marrying Anne to King Henry, the duke hoped to forge a Protestant alliance with England so he could gain access to Protestant allies off the continent.

In early 1539, two years into his widowhood, and encouraged by the promise of political support through the alliance with Cleves, Henry agreed to Cromwell starting marriage negotiations with the new Duke of Cleves, Anne's brother, Wilhelm. Henry also saw the negotiations as an opportunity to try and marry his eldest daughter by Katherine of Aragon, Mary, to Wilhelm of Cleves to further strengthen their alliance against the Catholic Holy Roman Emperor, Charles V. Poor Mary's marital prospects were rather blighted by the fact that Henry had bad-feeling towards both his daughters' mothers, and both Mary and Elizabeth's audacity at being born female. Henry's revenge had been to use an act of parliament to proclaim them both illegitimate. Nevertheless, Cromwell recruited two of his best men to carry out the diplomatic task of negotiating with Duke Wilhelm; they were Nicholas Wotton and Richard Beard. As negotiations for Henry's marriage furthered, Wilhelm became less enthusiastic at the prospect of marrying Lady Mary. Her illegitimate status and unflatering reports of her physical appearance and dull personality meant that soon the negotiations focused solely on the proposed union between Henry and Anne.

The summer was turning into autumn when the negotiations produced a drafted contract; however, Henry was unwilling to marry anyone without seeing a true likeness of them first. At the time, rumours had started to circulate around his court that Henry was having difficulty in 'rising to the occasion' in the royal bed chamber. Therefore, it is possible that he wanted to know that his new wife's appearance would help to encourage his passions before he committed to marriage. The sixteenth century equivalent of a photograph was a portrait and Henry sent the renowned renaissance portrait painter, Hans Holbein the Younger, to Cleves in order to capture the potential new queen's likeness for him. The resulting picture was clearly to his taste and the portrait was what finally convinced Henry to agree to the contract and take Anne as his fourth queen. The man trusted with sealing the negotiations and bringing them to a happy conclusion was Stephen Vaughan, a very able diplomat. Once the contract was signed, Vaughan stood in proxy for Henry at a betrothal ceremony held with Anne in Cleves. All that was left to do was to finalise the contract in London, on 4 October 1539.

If first impressions are anything to go by, Anne and Henry's marriage was doomed from the start. Anne's journey to her new life in England was delayed due to the problematic winter weather and Henry must have been very frustrated as he had been eager to meet his next queen in person. Fuelled by festive spirit and ideas of courtly love, Henry thought he would surprise his new bride before she reached London. On 1 January 1540, Anne and her party were staying at Rochester Abbey, where the king and several of his closest courtiers surprised Anne incognito. The Spanish ambassador Eustace Chapuys was present at the awkward first meeting and recorded the following:

> '[Henry] so went up into the chamber where the said Lady Anne was looking out the window to see the bull-baiting which was going on in the courtyard and suddenly he embraced and kissed her and showed her a token which the king had sent for her New Year's gift and she being abashed and not knowing who it was thanked him and so he spoke with her. But she regarded him little but always looked out the window.'

Poor Anne, she had been expecting to formally meet her new husband not have him surprise her by messing around like a young fool. She was clearly not enchanted by his sense of humour or person. In return, Henry seems to have found Anne too different in likeness from her portrait and was disappointed by her actual appearance. Unfortunately, or fortunately, depending how you see it, that Henry never fully got over this first disastrous meeting and the dent it made to his delicate male ego.

Two days later, on 3 January 1540, Henry officially met Anne's party at Blackheath near Greenwich. From Blackheath, they travelled together to the now lost Palace of Placentia to start the feasting and preparations for their full marriage ceremony. Henry behaved chivalrously in public towards Anne but once in private, he raged at Cromwell, demanding that he find a way to put a stop to the marriage before it was legally finalised. But even Henry knew that at this point within the marriage process, it would have been extremely insulting to his new Germanic allies to back out, and in the end, he forced himself to go through with his fourth marriage.

The final ceremony took place at the Palace of Placentia on 6 January 1540 and was led by the archbishop of Canterbury, Thomas Cranmer.

In the eyes of the church, although Henry and Anne had taken holy vows in front of God, they were not fully married until the union was consummated within the bedchamber. On the morning after the wedding night, Henry complained to Cromwell saying, 'I liked her before not well but I like her much worse'. The royal couple had failed to consummate the marriage thus giving both parties a possible loophole to end the union. Henry stated that 'saggy breasts' and 'body odour' were two of the reasons why he was turned off by Anne. Consequently, history has remembered Anne in these sexist and unkind ways despite the fact that independent sources have never cited such unkind remarks about her appearance or person. Anne was the only one of Henry's wives he had not met before he agreed to marry her, and physical attraction was clearly a very important factor in a wife for the aging king.

The marriage continued without further attempts at consummation until the early summer of 1540. The marriage had barely lasted six months and in that time, Cromwell had become the scapegoat for the disastrous union. Finally, the pretence came to an end on 24 June 1540, when Anne was asked to leave the royal court. Just over two weeks later, her marriage to the most notorious king in Europe legally ended in an annulment due to non-consummation of the union. Anne, unlike her predecessors, was wise enough to agree with Henry rather than fight him to remain married. By annulling their brief and awkward marriage, Anne not only kept her head, but she would go on to have a good platonic relationship with the often difficult Henry, and by default, she become part of the royal family. She also went on to gain financially from the separation, with several properties and estates being gifted to her from the crown. All in all, Anne did not do too badly out of her short marriage to Henry. It could be argued that she was the most successful of all his wives.

While Anne may have escaped Henry's displeasure, the royal match maker, Thomas Cromwell, was far less lucky. He found himself arrested and convicted of high treason and went to the block upon Tower Hill on the 28 July 1540, while Henry was in the process of marring his next wife, Catherine Howard.

During his six-month marriage to Anne, Henry had repeated history and taken a fancy to one of his queen's ladies-in-waiting, the very young and very pretty Catherine Howard. Catherine belonged to one of the most powerful and influential families who attended Henry's court. The Howards were related to Henry's second wife's family, the Boleyn's, through marriage. Like many young women from important and powerful families, Catherine was sent to court to serve the queen and to be introduced to society, in the hope that she would makes a good marriage. She entered service in her mid-teens, her exact date of birth is unknown, but it is thought she was around the age of 15 or 16 when Henry noticed her. In 1540, Henry was 46 while his youngest daughter little Lady Elizabeth was seven years of age. Henry was thirty years Catherine's senior, a disturbing age gap, made even worse when you realise that Catherine was not even a legal adult. Catherine's mother, Joyce Culpepper, had been an aunt to Anne Boleyn, thus making Catherine Howard first cousin once removed from little Elizabeth. In turn, this would make Henry her uncle once removed by marriage. If the age gap between Henry and Catherine had not been verging on indecent, then the proximity of their families and Catherine's family links with Elizabeth makes Henry's infatuation seem even more inappropriate to modern tastes and sensibilities.

Seeing that Henry was not remotely interested in poor Anne of Cleves, the power-hungry Howards saw the king's interest in Catherine and decided that this was an ideal opportunity for the family to regain influence and favour. The most prominent member of the Howard dynasty was Thomas Howard, 2nd Duke of Norfolk. The role of an aristocratic daughter during the sixteenth century was to be used as an advantageous pawn by her family. Catherine, who was barely into the first flushes of her womanhood, would become victim to her family's ambition and greed for power within the royal court.

As Henry's annulment to Anne was finalised, the king was in full pursuit of Catherine and she in turn, was encouraged by her family to flatter and welcome his majesty's growing interest in her. During their courtship, Henry granted Catherine expensive gifts including rich cloths and large profitable estates of land. Within a month of annulling his marriage to Anne, Henry and Catherine, had married on 28 July 1540.

During the next six months, Henry's fifth marriage seemed to be in a happy honeymoon period. Catherine was bestowed with gifts and new clothes from Henry and in the summer months they left London to undertake a royal progress around the home counties, stopping at Reading in Berkshire and Woking in Buckinghamshire. The year ended with luxurious Christmas celebrations hosted at Hampton Court Palace. Henry, however, had become moody and bad tempered with his counsellors. This was partly due to his infected leg giving him continual discomfort. Some historians even suggest that this shift in mood was due to the king deeply regretting the execution of his long time, loyal ally, Thomas Cromwell. This must have been very hard for the young Queen Catherine. It is not known if Henry took his dark moods and temper out on his new bride in private but life as teenage queen cannot have been easy with a fat, smelly and grumpy, middle-aged man.

It is thought that about nine months into her marriage to Henry, the young, foolhardy queen started her first treasonous liaison with Thomas Culpepper, a very distant relation. These clandestine meetings were aided by someone with experience in such matters, Jane Boleyn, the Viscountess of Rochford, who had been the unfortunate wife of George Boleyn, the brother and supposed lover of Queen Anne. Before her marriage to Henry, Catherine had not been virtuous and maidenly. Upon the death of her mother when Catherine was about five, she and some of her siblings had been sent to live with their paternal grandmother, the Dowager Duchess of Norfolk. The dowager duchess was not as observant as she should have been with the young pretty wards in her care. Catherine would later confess, during her trial, that when she was 13, she had engaged in sexual behaviour with her music tutor, Henry Madox.

Catherine's next known sexual relations happened with her grandmother's personal secretary, Francis Dereham. Aged 15, she and Dereham became intimately acquainted but this relationship was brought to a close when the dowager duchess discovered what they had been up to; Dereham was promptly sent to Ireland and Catherine was sent from the frying pan and into the fire, when her uncle, the Duke of Norfolk, found his wayward niece a place at court within the new queen's household, as a lady-in-waiting.

Unfortunately for Catherine, her past behaviour from the time she had lived as a ward of her grandmother was widely known, and when she became queen, former acquaintances armed with this knowledge of her past, blackmailed Catherine in exchange for favours. One such individual who bribed Catherine was John Lascelles whose sister, Mary, had also been a fellow ward with Catherine within the dowager duchess's household. Mary Lascelles had seen Catherine carrying on inappropriately with Francis Dereham. Unwisely, the attempt to blackmail the queen to gain a position at court was ignored and the spurned Lascelles took his revenge on Catherine by telling all he knew about her promiscuous past to Thomas Cranmer. Cranmer was the right person to tell, for he was a new reformist Protestant just like Thomas Cromwell and Anne Boleyn had been. The Howard family had remained firmly Catholic during the English reformation and Cranmer was looking for a way to bring down the powerful Catholic Duke of Norfolk, and John Lascelles was handing him the perfect ammunition to do this.

Henry and Catherine were on the Northern Progress at the time Cramer started to make investigations into Catherine's former life and sexual conduct. The Viscountess Rochford was cornered and once again found herself informing on a queen and one of her relatives' behaviour to a royal investigator. She had seen what happened to her former husband, George Boleyn and her sister-in-law and she had clearly decided that the best thing to keep her head attached to her body was to tell Cranmer the truth. She revealed to the archbishop that Thomas Culpepper had been sneaking in and out of the queen's apartments at various times of day and night. Culpepper's quarters were searched which revealed that he'd kept a love letter from Catherine. This was enough to execute an arrest warrant for Henry's fifth wife. Cranmer presented the arrest warrant to Henry on 1 November 1541 while he was praying in his chapel. For Henry it must have felt like history was repeating itself and to make things worse, Catherine was part of the same family. This time, Henry was not going to show his young wife any mercy.

Catherine's fall was swift. She was initially held at the bishop's Winchester Palace where she was ruthlessly questioned by Cranmer. It is worth noting that Catherine was still a teenage girl and had not received the same educational training as Elizabeth and so the Archbishop, not unsurprisingly, found her in a state of sheer panic. Her anguish was such that he feared that she might attempt to take her life. Throughout her interrogations Catherine made one fatal error, she denied that there had been any pre-contract of marriage between herself and Dereham, prior to her marriage to Henry. Had she said that there was and found evidence of the agreement either in writing or a witness, Henry may have been persuaded to annul their marriage on the grounds that she was not free to marry him and might have banished Catherine from court in disgrace and poverty, but at least she would have survived. Maybe Catherine refused to say anything as she feared the wrath of her mighty uncle, the Duke of Norfolk, or perhaps she hoped that by denying there had been a pre-existing contract of marriage between herself and Dereham, she might be able save her first love's life, as teenage girls tend to over romanticise such things.

On 23 November 1541, Catherine was formally striped of her title of Queen of England. She was moved from the custody of the bishop within his Winchester Palace in Southwark, to the former convent of Syon, which had also fallen under the Henrician reformation during the dissolution of the monasteries. There is a certain irony in imprisoning a fallen queen, charged with adultery and high treason within a fallen former convent.

The trials of Francis Dereham, who had not touched the queen while she had been married to Henry and that of Thomas Culpepper, both took place on 1 December. It was little more than a formality, both young men were found guilty of high treason. Ten days later, both men were executed at Tyburn. Thomas Culpepper was dispatched by beheading due to his place in society. But poor Francis Dereham, was shown no mercy as he faced the cruel death of being hung, drawn and quartered for simply having had a consensual fling with a young girl before she had even gone to court, let alone married a king. It was a cruel ending for what many may consider no crime.

Catherine's fate was less certain as she remained in prison without being tried for her crimes. This was a cruel thing to do as it may have given her false hope that the delay meant that Henry had forgiven her. Early in 1542, on the 29 January, Henry's Parliament issued a Bill of Attainer against the former queen. This bill meant that her guilt had already been proven and that she had been legally found guilty without the need of a trial. She was removed from the former Abbey of Syon on the 10 February when she was relocated to the Tower of London. On her journey up the River Thames she would have seen the heads of both Dereham and Culpepper displayed upon London Bridge. She was only to be held at The Tower for three days.

On the evening of the 12 February, Catherine requested that an execution block be brought to her cell, so that she could practise how she needed to lay her head upon it. At 7.00 am, on the 13 February, Catherine was led to Tower Green within the precinct of the famous Norman fortress. Catherine's end was swift, as it only took one strike of the axe to remove her head from her body. Shortly after, Jane Boleyn, the former Viscountess of Rochford, followed the fate of her late husband and sister-in-law to the executioner's block. Her crime had been aiding the queen in committing adultery and failing to disclose knowledge of the queen's behaviour.

The fates of these two very different women in Elizabeth's childhood would have made an impact on the young Elizabeth as she was a very intelligent girl and she would have understood as well as learnt from the successes and mistakes made by Anne of Cleves and Catherine Howard. The fourth and fifth wives of her father, were opposites on how to survive marriage to Henry. Anne had come from a controlling and patriarchal German family and although Henry may not have been of ideal marriage material, the marriage allowed her to escape her family and by co-operating with Henry she was able to stay in England as well as keeping her head; Anne had given Henry what he wanted, and in return, she was rewarded well. Elizabeth herself used this tact with her sister Mary over the issue of religion - she passively followed the rule in order to survive and didn't argue over the terms of Mary's will requesting the nation remain Roman Catholic - she knew Mary could not do anything from her grave. Anne's skill was all about understanding when it is necessary to compromise in order to reach your final goal.

Catherine Howard was in comparison, arguably Henry's least successful wife and the unluckiest. Her age and lack of maturity, as well as her naivety played major roles in her tragic story. She was also indiscreet and trusted too much in the wrong people. Although Elizabeth could be indiscreet in her close friendship with Robert Dudley after she ascended the throne, she even favoured him by moving his rooms next to hers, she did distance herself from him, when there was hints of scandal surrounding him after the death of his first wife Amy Robsart. She was also careful about how flirtatious she was with him in public. Elizabeth, when she was queen, also expected loyalty and trust from her women and her council all of whom were carefully chosen by herself. It is not surprising Elizabeth is famously said to have asserted 'my dogs wear my collars'. This comment was aimed at Henry Clifford for accepting an honour from the French without her expressed permission. Catherine Howard was also proof that being a young woman of a certain class during the sixteenth century made you extremely vulnerable to the whims and control of your family and especially powerful men - Elizabeth never allowed herself to become used as political pawn in the same way as Catherine Howard and many others had done.

1543: The Marriage of Henry VIII & Katherine Parr

The last of Henry VIII's wives, Katherine Parr can be seen as the most important in terms of the creation of Elizabeth as a queen. Even as a sixteenth century woman, Katherine had managed to achieve a lot in her thirty-six years of life, and she was the most influential of Henry's wives during Elizabeth's adolescence.

Katherine came from a prominent and noble family with ancestry connecting her to Edward III. It is estimated that she was born in the summer of 1512 in Cumbria to Sir Thomas Parr and his wife Maud (nee Green). Amongst the titles Thomas Parr held was the office of the Sheriff of Nottingham. Her mother Maud had been a lady-in-waiting to Henry's first wife, Katherine of Aragon, who was also Katherine's godmother. Katherine was lucky, despite losing her father at an early age, that she was still able to enjoy a renaissance education that had taught her Latin, French and Italian. Her education stopped when she was 17, and she married the first of her four husbands, Sir Edward Burgh.

Edward Burgh was in his early to mid-twenties when the pair wed in 1529; their marriage lasted around three years. During that time, Edward worked as a Justice of the Peace and for a short time the couple lived with Sir Edward's family. It was not a particularly happy time, but the couple soon moved to their own private residence in Kirton Lindsey in Lincolnshire. Edward died in spring 1533, without the couple ever having children, and Katherine received part of her dowry back by the way of the incomes from two of her father-in-law's properties in the south of England.

Katherine was now in her early twenties and did not remain a widow for long. In the summer of 1534, just over a year after her first husband had died, she would marry John Neville, the 3rd Baron of Latimer.

In just over a year, Katherine had significantly climbed the social ladder of Tudor England. Katherine's life as Lady Latimer was greatly different from that of her first marriage. As well as gaining an older husband, Katherine also gained stepchildren. Latimer was also a cousin to her father, which to twenty-first century sensibilities seems like a strange arrangement.

It was an eventful marriage with her husband held prisoner from October 1536 until April the following year by Catholic rebels as part of the Lincolnshire Rising. Katherine then found herself hostage along with her stepchildren in 1537, at the peak of the Rising of the North in Yorkshire. Their marriage, though eventful and by all accounts happy, did not produce any children and by 1542, Lord Latimer's health had started to decline. He died on 2 March 1543, aged 49-years-old. For an arranged marriage, the couple were at least fond of each other and Katherine was affectionate and caring towards her stepdaughter who she took over as guardian of, upon Latimer's death. Katherine now found herself a wealthy woman and a widow for a second time.

Katherine was now in her late twenties. Widowed noblewomen of the sixteenth century had several options: remarry, enter a convent (although that was less of an option in post reformation England) or try to gain access to a royal household; Katherine chose to become a member of Lady Mary's household. This decision would change her life once again, as it was here that she would meet both of her last two husbands, Henry VIII and Thomas Seymour. Having been dutiful twice, Katherine must have wanted to choose a husband of her own for her third marriage and she started to pay court to Thomas Seymour, the younger brother of the late Queen Jane and uncle to little Prince Edward. However, her choice of husband would have to wait, as Thomas Seymour was not the only man Katherine had caught the attention of - the now notorious Henry VIII was not a man to displease or turn down.

Henry was now in his fifties and in declining health. He was looking for companionship and a nurse in a wife rather than a potential lover. His fifth wife, Catherine Howard had been young, immature and had made a fool out of Henry and his vanity. In comparison, Katherine Parr was older, and she had been widowed. She was also educated, attractive and had the experience of nursing an older husband in ill health, it is little wonder that Henry thought that she would make him a perfect wife.

The problem of Thomas Seymour was swiftly resolved when Henry sent him to Europe on diplomatic business and Henry set out to woo Lady Katherine Latimer. It is hard to imagine how Katherine felt, Henry had married five times, he had previously executed two of those women and was by this point a temperamental, fat and, due to an ulcer on his lower leg, a smelly old man. The thought of marrying such a notorious man must have been intimidating. Whether through compassion or a sense of duty, Katherine accepted Henry's proposal and married him in a small private ceremony held at Hampton Court Palace, on 12 July 1543.

One of the first actions as queen that Katherine undertook was to help unite Henry with his daughters, Lady Mary and Lady Elizabeth. The result of this action was the Third Succession Act of 1543, being passed, which put both Mary and Elizabeth back in line to the throne although it did not remove their illegitimate status. Neither of Henry's daughters lived with him and Katherine encouraged the king to make the effort to get to know his estranged offspring.

In that same year, Katherine published her first book. Books were rare in the sixteenth century and to write and publish a book was a rare achievement for a man let alone a woman during this time. The majority of women at this time were illiterate and barely able to write their own names. Katherine's first work was published anonymously. Two years later, the work was republished under the title of *Prayers and Meditations* and the queen was happy to publicly put her name to the republished work. This accomplishment by a woman within her family circle must have left an impression on Lady Elizabeth who was also a well-educated young woman.

Another of Katherine's accomplishments was persuading Henry to make her his regent while he was away in France, at the end of 1544. The position of regent would also have been another positive reinforcement of strong female empowerment for Elizabeth to witness at an impressionable age in her early teenage years.

Katherine was also a survivor. In 1546, she learnt that Henry had issued a warrant for her arrest on the grounds of her reformist Protestant beliefs. Katherine was able to act swiftly; unlike her predecessors, she was able to mediate with her husband and successfully argued that her only motivation for being outspoken on her religious views with him was to help take his mind off the constant discomfort and pain. After their reconciliation, Katherine was more guarded in expressing her religious opinion but in private, she worked on a second work, called *The Lamentation of a Sinne*r. This work was subsequently not published until after the death of Henry in 1547. Henry too changed slightly towards his wife and this is evident as she had fully expected to have been appointed Prince Edward's regent after Henry's death. However, in his last will, Henry had changed his mind and made Edward's uncle, Edward Seymour and a council of men in charge of his son's reign, until his majority rather than Katherine.

One of the biggest interests that Elizabeth shared with her last stepmother was her religious conviction in support of the new reformist faith. In 1546, Lady Elizabeth gave her father a hand-written and embroidered translation of *Prayers and Meditations* translated into Italian, French and Latin. Quite an accomplishment for a teenage girl.

Henry VIII died on 18 January 1547. Katherine now became the Dowager Queen of England and she chose to remain within the royal court until her stepson, Prince Edward was officially crowned. She was allowed to keep her robes and jewels for her lifetime as she had been the only one of Henry's wives to have survived her queenship. She moved from court to her in manor located in Chelsea, which was in the sixteenth century was a small rural village on the outskirts of London. Before long, she had resumed her relationship with Thomas Seymour and went on to marry him in secret months after Henry's death.

The marriage of Katherine to Henry was arguably the most important and influential event to have happened during Elizabeth's youth. Katherine acted as the mother that had been missing from her life. She was a positive role model who shared many of the characteristics that would go on to define the queen that Elizabeth became: Intelligent, Protestant, strong and fiercely independent. It was also in Katherine's care after her father's death that Elizabeth learnt another important life lesson; distance yourself from scandal involving men.

1547: The Death of Henry VIII

The death of a parent is a life changing moment for us all but when your parent is a monarch your life changes both privately and publicly. This was most definitely the case for Henry VIII's three children, Edward, Mary and Elizabeth. Each would take the crown and make their own mark upon history.

Towards the end of 1546, Henry's health started to decline steadily. Towards the end of his reign, Henry had morphed into large man, a major contributing factor to his great size was his lack of mobility due to pain caused from an ulcerated leg caused by a wound sustained during a jousting accident in 1536. This infected wound was not just a source of pain but was also extremely pungent and would have contributed to his cantankerous mood swings and short temper. Another factor that would have affected his weight gain and health in general were his eating habits. A rich diet made up of a lot of meat, refined white breads, cheeses, dairy products and surprisingly vast quantities of fruit and veg both fresh, raw and cooked as well as preserved, through drying or the making of jams or marmalades. The king was fond of his food, and as a consequence, many of the health issues we associate with obesity today would have affected Henry's health especially near the end of his reign.

The real decline in Henry's health happened during the festive season of 1546, which was when his last will and testimony was revised and authenticated on 30 December and placed in a sealed box. The will was authenticated by a signature stamp rather than signed by the king; this was the Tudor equivalent of the E signature we use today. This had become a common practice within the Henrician administration from September 1545. The seal of such documents was delegated to his trusted counsellors and secretaries. In order to prevent the misuse of such a powerful seal, the clerks and counsellors kept a record of who, why and for what the stamp was used to officiate. It is due to this surviving record that we know

Henry created a new will at this time. Despite his physical decline, Henry continued to keep a firm grip on his regal power for almost another month after his last will was drawn up. This reluctance to show weakness and give in to the fragility and the mortality of being a human was something his youngest daughter, Elizabeth inherited from her father as she too refused to give in to her mortality until the last month of her life in spring 1603.

But even kings are mortal and on 27 January the end was approaching. When the Archbishop of Canterbury, Thomas Cranmer was summoned to administer the last rites, Henry was no longer able to speak. When asked during the sacrament to put his trust in Christ, the dying Henry squeezed the Archbishop's hand in response. At 2.00 am on 28 January 1547, Henry VIII died in his sleep, leaving his country in the hands of his nine-year-old son, Prince Edward. Elizabeth was 13 years-old at the time.

At the time of her father's death, Lady Mary, Henry's eldest daughter, was into her thirties, and although she had been reinstated to the line of succession through the Third Succession Act of 1542, Mary was second in line to the throne and would only reign if Edward didn't produce legitimate heirs of his own. This was all due to Mary being a female. Mary must have worried about her half-brother's reign as she, like her late Spanish mother, Katherine of Argon, was Roman Catholic while Edward was resolutely Protestant. Unlike his father, Edward had been brought up as a Protestant and educated by reformist Protestant tutors. Mary must have worried that her younger half-brother and his regency council might impose their religious convictions upon her, thus endangering her immortal soul.

At the time of her father's death, Lady Elizabeth was residing at Enfield Manor. The royal children were told together of their father's death. Elizabeth's main concern at this point would have been about where her brother's regency council thought it suitable to send her to live or marry, as both of her parents were now dead.

The new king would be at the mercy of his ambitious, political and power-hungry maternal family; the Seymours. Throughout the late king Henry's reign, the Seymour family had sparred for power within the Henrician court with other noble families including the notorious Boleyn and Howard clans. Ultimately, the Seymour family knew that regardless of whether the tempestuous Henry favoured them or not, they would ultimately win the power game, as long as their sister's son, Prince Edward was successful in succeeding to the English throne, and in January 1547, the Seymour's got their moment of glory. This was their opportunity to wield power by manipulating the young King Edward. It took little more than forty-eight hours for the Seymour brothers to have tightened their grip on power and to have ensnared their nephew, the new king. The elder of the Seymour brothers, Edward, the Duke of Somerset, had been made de facto regent for the young king. It was this position that would drive a wedge between the Seymour dukes, ultimately leading to both men dying as traitors in their pursuit of power. The creation of Edward Seymour as the Lord Protector of the new monarch was not exactly what the late Henry had stipulated he wanted to happen in his will. Henry had in fact wanted a council of sixteen men to rule, guide and train Edward until he came of age at 18. Henry did not want the influence of just one person or family to dominate or influence his son.

It is very possible that Henry may have discussed this with his last wife, Katherine Parr, who immediately after the death of her husband did not sign her documents Dowager Queen, the traditional title of a widowed consort but 'Katherine Quene [sic] Regent'; implying that she was under the impression that she would play a major role in the regency of the young monarch.

Prior to his funeral, the late King Henry lay in state for ten days embalmed within the Privy Chamber of Whitehall Palace. On Valentine's day 1547, the massive logistical task of moving his large body from Westminster to his final resting place in St George's chapel within Windsor Castle began. The large hearse was accompanied in regal style by a thousand horsemen. This final journey took two days and the party stopped overnight at Edward Seymour's home, Syon, before continuing with its mournful procession.

The funeral service was held in the royal chapel of St George within the grounds of Windsor Castle. The mass was officiated by Catholic Bishop Gardiner, with the traditional Latin liturgy. This was quite an irony as Henry was the monarch who had started the English Reformation. After the mass, Henry's large lead-lined coffin was interred into a crypt with his third wife and the mother of the new king, Jane Seymour. Now that the late king was at peace it was time to crown his son and heir. This would have been especially important to the king's uncles as they wanted to secure their power and influence over Edward. Therefore the sooner he was crowned, the less likely they were to experience a struggle for power from any other royal dynasty, either at home or abroad.

As per tradition, Edward was moved to the Tower of London before his coronation. Today the Tower of London is best known and remembered as a notorious prison and execution site for treasonous criminals, however it was also a royal palace, the royal treasury, an armoury, a barracks and was home to a host of exotic animals that formed the royal menagerie until 1830, when the royal animals were relocated to Regent's Park and formed the foundation of London Zoo.

On the day before his coronation the boy king went on a hastily organised progress around the city of London so that some of his subjects could see their new king and enjoy free wine and pageantry. On 20 February, only five days after his father's funeral, Edward was brought from the Tower of London by royal barge to Westminster Abbey to formalise his new role and hopefully continue the Tudor line. It is important to note that Edward VI's coronation ceremony would break the tradition and changes were made due to the young age of the king as well as to reflect the religious reforms that had happened since the last English coronation. Previous coronation days lasted for a gruelling twelve hours or more. That is a very long day for an adult to undertake let alone a child, and so the festivities and the service were shortened to seven hours. Then there was the issue of the crown, although the traditional crowns were used during the coronation ceremony, a new crown especially designed for Edward, was made to ensure it was both light and fitted his small head.

The biggest changes were the alterations to the wording of the coronation service itself. These changes reflected the reforms within the English church. This was a strong indicator that Edward would continue with the Protestant reforms as the new monarch. During the services homily, the Archbishop of Canterbury, Thomas Cranmer, explained these changes to the congregation present. Edward was expected to be a Christian king and to rule using his own understanding of the Bible and God's word, and to not be directed and controlled by the Pope in Rome. This pious and Protestant start to his reign, would continue throughout Edward's brief time as monarch. Unlike his father, Edwards regency council would shape this new form of English reformist Christian doctrine.

During her brother's reign, Elizabeth would have witnessed how his faith influenced all aspects of his role as king and seen both the positive and negative effects of this influence. She would also experience the negative impact of her half-sister's Catholic reign and both these experiences gave Elizabeth a more tolerant view of faith when she finally ascended to the throne herself in 1558.

1548: The Scandal of Thomas Seymour

Upon the death of her father Henry VIII, at the beginning of 1547, Elizabeth was only just a teenager and residing at a manor called Enfield located in the north of London. The new king, Edward VI was brought to Enfield Manor by his uncle Edward Seymour and it was here that Seymour informed the royal children that their father had died. Both children were said to have been reduced to tears by the news of their father's death. Henry had been a remote father who had been worshiped due to his role as king and although he had been distant, for Elizabeth, Henry had at least been the one person she could trust to not let anyone else harm her; now she found herself at the mercy of her brother and his regency council.

As the dowager queen, Katherine Parr was the last of Elizabeth's stepmothers and they had always had a close relationship and corresponded with each other frequently. Katherine had been instrumental in restoring both Mary and Elizabeth to the line of succession in the new succession act of 1542.

Edward was now King of England, but Elizabeth was still a minor without an official guardian. Her stepsister had now become second in line to the throne and had been living with Katherine Parr. Mary quickly became offended by Katherine's swift and clandestine romance with Thomas Seymour, who she married soon after the death of her father, the late King Henry and left Katherine's home in Chelsea. Elizabeth subsequently moved from Enfield Manor to Katherine Parr's Chelsea manor in spring 1547. The manor in Chelsea had been granted to Katherine by the late king three years earlier, and Elizabeth moved in before Katherine married her half-brother's uncle, Thomas Seymour.

Elizabeth was also joined at Chelsea by her first cousin once removed, Lady Jane Grey. Jane was younger than Elizabeth by three years and she also had a distant claim to the English throne due to the Third Succession

Act of parliament in 1542. In the terms agreed by Henry VIII, if his three children had no descendants to inherit the crown, then the throne should pass to the heirs of his younger sister Mary. Jane was Mary's eldest granddaughter. Lady Jane remained with Katherine's household when they moved into Seymour Place and Thomas Seymour brought Jane's wardship for the huge sum of £6,000. Having Jane Grey join the new Parr-Seymour household was probably a politically motivated move. The swift remarriage of the dowager queen was somewhat scandalous and done in an indecent haste. By having two royal women, who were both relatively close to the line of succession within the Seymour-Parr household would ensure that both Katherine and Seymour would need to have access to the newly established court of the new king. The second and probably biggest reason why Thomas brought Jane's wardship was that there was serious rivalry between himself and his elder brother Edward Seymour.

There was of course the natural rivalry between ambitious siblings, but this rivalry became a personal grudge when Edward was made Protector of King Edward VI. As Protector, Edward Seymour now had the most power within the royal court and a greater influence over the new king, their nephew. Thomas Seymour had no reason to feel jealous of his older brother, as he was also part of the regency council that helped the nine-year-old king; he was also granted the title of First Baron Seymour of Sudeley, was bestowed the official position of Lord High Admiral and, in addition, was made a Knight of the Garter. Relations between the two Seymour brothers were not helped when Thomas had clandestinely married Katherine in undignified haste. Thomas made things worse by deciding to appeal straight to his nephew, the king, rather than going through the regency council and speaking with his brother.

To get access to the young king, Thomas needed to bribe one of his nephew's Gentlemen of the Privy Chamber, John Fowler. Seymour bribed Fowler £10, a substantial sum in the sixteenth century. Seymour needed Fowler to ask the king if he thought it strange that he was not married and who he thought would be a suitable bride for his uncle Thomas. The ploy worked and the young king agreed his uncle should have a wife. The first of Edward's suggestions however did not meet with Thomas's approval. The young king first thought of his fleeting German stepmother, Anne of Cleves, as a possible wife. His next suggestion was even more unappealing to his uncle, as Edward proposed his elder stepsister Mary. The young king's motives for suggesting his older sibling may have been in the hope that Seymour might be able to convert his Catholic sibling to the Protestant faith. Upon this suggestion, Seymour decided to help his nephew along and he advised Fowler to suggest his last stepmother Katherine as a suitable choice. Edward agreed and Thomas had got what he wanted without having to go through the regency council or seek his elder brothers approval.

There does not seem to be a consensus amongst Tudor scholars about when Katherine legally married Thomas Seymour. This is mainly because the marriage was held in secrecy due to its sensitive nature and her lacking permissions from the new king. Dr David Starkey judges that the marriage between Katherine and Seymour took place in mid-April 1547 and this seems to make sense given the timeline of Thomas's manipulation of his nephew via John Fowler. This resulted in a letter to Katherine from young Edward dated at the end of May.

In an age before effective contraception, it was not long before Katherine, then aged 34, fell pregnant. No children had materialised from her first three marriages, but this seems to prove that the fault was not due to her biology but those of her previous husbands. Today, pregnancy in your mid-thirties is considered late but it is still relatively safe for a healthy woman. However, during the sixteenth century, pregnancy at this age was considered far more perilous for both mother and child.

It was during Katherine's pregnancy that Thomas Seymour would start to behave in such a way that history would rightly question his motivations towards the young teenage Elizabeth. In the state papers, there are hints of inappropriate behaviour by Seymour as he enters the Elizabeth's room in the morning 'bare-legged'. The following quotation is an eyewitness account from Kat Ashley, who witnessed this over familiarity between Seymour and Elizabeth:

> 'He would come many mornings into the said Lady Elizabeth's chamber, before she were ready, and sometimes before she did rise. And if she were up, he would bid her good morrow and ask how she did, and strike her upon the back or on the buttocks familiarly, and so forth through his lodgings... and if she were in her bed, he would put open the curtains' (State papers Haynes ed).

It has also been hinted that Katherine herself joined in the 'games' when her husband was tickling her stepdaughter while she was still in bed. Katherine is also said to have held Elizabeth in the gardens as Seymour 'cut her dress in a hundred pieces' *(Starkey, Elizabeth p.69, Jenkins E, Elizabeth the great, p. 27)*. This behavior, however, came to an abrupt end in May 1548 when Elizabeth found herself sent from the care of her stepmother to the wardship of Sir Anthony Denny, who lived in Cheshunt, in order to ensure that there was no risk to Elizabeth's reputation due to this over familiarity between herself and Seymour. Just after leaving the Seymour household, Elizabeth wrote to her last stepmother in a grateful but worried tone.

> 'Although I could not be plentiful in giving thanks for the manifold kindness received at your highness' hand at my departure, yet I am somewhat to be borne withal, for truly I was replete with sorrow to depart from your highness especially leaving you undoubtful of health."The Princess signs off the letter "From Cheshunt, this present Saturday. Your highness' humble daughter, Elizabeth.' (Porter L, Katherine the Queen, pp.313-4)

It is possible that at first, Elizabeth might have been flattered by the attentions of an older, handsome man, but in my opinion, as time wore on, she probably didn't welcome Seymour's flirtations, probably fearing for her reputation.

Katherine gave birth to her daughter, Mary Seymour, on 30 August 1548. However, Katherine did not survive to see her daughter grow up. Like her sister-in-law Jane, a decade before her, Katherine died six days after the delivery of her daughter on 7 September 1548, of childbed complications. Elizabeth never saw her favourite stepmother alive again.

Seymour may have mourned his wife, but this did not stop him from politically plotting against his brother. However, eventually, Thomas Seymour did make the fatal mistake of being caught manipulating his nephew King Edward against his brother, the Lord Protector. The Lord Protector's role was supposed to be kept in check by the regency council. Thomas Seymour was able to undermine his brother and win the favour of his nephew, the king with money and gifts.

The regency council started to fear what Thomas Seymour may do. One of these fears was that he may go as far as to kidnap the king and use this leverage to force change in the government. Seymour was also a potential danger to national security as he held the position of the Lord Admiral of the English Royal Navy, a risky position for someone who was openly against the current government. The event that finally caused Seymour to be arrested happened on 16 January 1549 when he was caught breaking into the king's bedchamber at Hampton Court Palace. This was a massive step too far for both his brother the Lord Protector and the regency council which was now forced to arrest him.

Due to her association with Seymour when she lived with Katherine Parr, Elizabeth found herself a suspect and in danger for the first time since her father's death; unfortunately, this would not be the last time danger fell upon her before she would become queen. Nearly two years after the death of Henry VIII, Elizabeth's companion and confident Kat Ashley, who had been with her young charge in the Seymour household, was taken into custody. It was during her confinement and interrogation that Ashley divulged the behaviour of Seymour and Katherine towards Elizabeth while in their care. This evidence did not help the reputation of Thomas Seymour with the regency council. The consequences of Kat Ashley's testimonial resulted in Lady Elizabeth facing questions about her conduct by Robert Tyrwhitt. Tyrwhitt and his wife had both been part of the Parr/Seymour household and would have been aware of the scandalous behaviour of Seymour towards Elizabeth while she lived there. During the questioning, the teenage Elizabeth held firm. All she confirmed was what Kat Ashley had said about Seymour's inappropriate behaviour. Even as a teenager, Elizabeth proved that she was a skilled survivor and could keep a cool head at a time of personal danger. She wrote to the Lord Protector, asking that he disregard the scandalous rumour that she was 'in the Tower with child by my Lord Admiral' (Haynes, Burghley State Papers p.89) and she hoped that the regency council would officially quash these untrue rumours. This was both a confident and bold move for an inexperienced teenage under official suspicion.

Thomas Seymour was found guilty of thirty-three counts of high treason in February 1549. He faced executed by beheading on Tower Hill on 20 March 1549. Kat Ashley was eventually released from The Tower in early March, weeks prior to Seymour's execution. The eminent Tudor historian Dr David Starkey evaluates this episode in Elizabeth's life well by saying that this is the point in the teenage Elizabeth's life when she finally grew up and entered adulthood in the most brutal of ways. *(Starkey, Elizabeth, p.76)* Her life would be dangerous and at points, she would find herself scarily close to death. Her life would not become stable again until she became queen, in November 1558.

1549: The Common Book of Prayer & The Prayer Book Rebellion

During the summer of 1549 (6 June - 17 August) King Edward's religious reforms relating to the introduction of the Common Book of Prayers caused such anger that Catholics in England's West Country took part in what became known as the Prayer Book Rebellion. Both the force of these doctrinal changes and the violent and brutal suppression of the rebels was just as bloodthirsty and vicious as the actions of the king's stepsister Mary's persecution of Protestants was to be during her short reign; yet these events in Edward's reign are widely forgotten about or are simply not considered to have been not as bloody as the behaviour of Mary because Edward was a king rather than a queen.

Civil unrest had been building up for eighteen months before the rebellion. It began when the Duke of Somerset appointed William Body to ensure that all iconography, shrines and religious practices considered 'too Catholic' were removed and stopped within the south west of England. This was a fatal appointment as William Body was found murdered on 5 April 1548. The crown soon discovered that it could only quash the unrest with the support of the local gentry. And those in authority liked to make examples of those who had fallen foul of the new rules.

This rebellion started because Somerset and the regency council ruled that the new Common Book of Prayer was to become mandatory in acts of worship within England and Wales on the first Sunday after Whitsunday. This was an attempt to finally wipe away the remaining parishes still celebrating mass in the Catholic tradition of Latin rather than English. The change had been formally made law under the Act of Uniformity.

Trouble started in the south west of England within one congregation, in the small village of Sampford Courtenay in Devon. The parishioners insisted that their priest continue to use the Latin service instead of complying with the new law. The local Justice of the Peace heard of the congregation's protests and came with the local militia to the next service. This action was to ensure that the parish was following the new law. After the service finished, a scuffle took place outside the church between the congregation and the militia and the fisticuffs quickly escalated resulting in the death of one of the congregation.

The death after the service and the anger over having to change their religious service prompted the people of Sampford Courtenay to take their protest to the nearest big city - Exeter. Word reached the city of the protesters' advance and the city's defensive gates were closed, which in turn resulted in a siege. News of the protest and siege spread throughout the West Country and a group of unhappy and frustrated Cornish men met on Bodmin Moor and started to attack the local gentry who were complying with the new law. Word of this unrest got back to the Duke of Somerset in London who deployed a member of the regency council, Sir John Russell, to the south west along with fighting mercenaries in an attempt to quash the rebellion before it spread further. On the 28 July, the two sides met face to face for the first of several battles. This first engagement was known as the Battle of Fenny Bridge. Neither side was able to claim victory so it became somewhat inevitable that the two sides would need to meet again before the rebellion was suppressed.

They next met seven days later on 4 August in a local area known as Woodbury Common. This clash also failed to create a definitive winner although the king's side did take substantial numbers of prisoners from the rebel cause. This forced the hand of the rebels who decided to attack the royal force again on the following day, the 5 August, in the small village of Cyst St Mary. This clash was far bloodier, and even more rebels were captured by Russell's men, approximately an additional nine hundred were taken prisoner. With no firm base in the south west and nowhere to hold the men captive, Russell needed to find a way to deal with the captured men. After the clash at Cyst St Mary, the prisoners were taken to the local heath where they were executed for treason without any formal trial. Nine hundred men had their throats cut in little over a quarter of an hour; making this little more than a massacre. The following day, the rebels once again attacked the royal forces and a further two thousand men died.

In the days that followed the final clash, Russell had begun to think that the rebellion was over, and he was able to liberate the city of Exeter from the five-week siege that it had been under. However, he got intelligence on 16 August that the rebels were once again regrouping in the village of Sampford Courtenay where the initial protest had started several weeks before. Russell and his mercenaries fought the remaining rebels who finally surrendered when they realised they had no hope in winning. It is thought that five and a half thousand men lost their lives in the Prayer Book Rebellion during the summer of 1549.

The killing however did not stop there. Following the end of the rebellion, trials and executions took place of the remaining leaders who had not been captured or killed in the fighting. This was one of the bloodiest episodes of the later Tudor monarchs and one of the least well-known. The number of Catholic and conservative Anglicans that lost their lives during the Prayer Book Rebellion was far higher than those who were persecuted and executed for Protestantism under Mary Tudor, who would go on to be remembered in history as 'Bloody Mary' for her actions.

The Prayer Book Rebellion would have been an important event in Elizabeth's life during the reign of her brother Edward as she was able to witness first-hand what happens when religious reform and intolerance spills into unrest and then rebellion, which is always a threat to a young monarch, especially a queen.

1553: The Premature Death of Edward VI - The Tudor's Last King

Although Henry VIII was the monarch to have started the reformation within England, it was during the reign of Edward VI, his son, that a more reformist doctrine entered the new English church's liturgy. Edward VI's regency council had been chosen as Henry thought that these men were more likely to work for the new king rather than for their own advancement or profit. Amongst their number were two of the late king's favourites - Stephen Gardiner and Henry Howard. King Henry had grossly underestimated the ambition of his son's maternal uncles, Thomas and Edward Seymour. Unwittingly, Henry had chosen men who felt that his reformation had failed to fully reform the English church. This of course is unsurprising as Henry's motives for introducing reform to England were for personal reasons not religious conviction.

The sixteen men named in Henry VIII's will as the members of his son's regency council were Edward Seymour; Duke of Somerset (Lord Protector, Military leader and uncle to King Edward), John Dudley; Viscount Lisle (Military Leader & courtier), Sir William Paget (politician), Sir Anthony Browne (courtier), Thomas Bromley (Chief Justice of the Kings Bench), Thomas Cramner (Archbishop of Canterbury), Sir Anthony Denny (courtier), Sir William Herbert (Courtier), Sir Edward Montague (Chief Justice of the Common Pleas), William Paulet, Baron St John of Basing (politician), Sir Edward North (Lawyer), Lord John Russell (Naval Admiral), Nicolas Wotton (diplomat), Thomas Wriothesley (courtier), Sir Edward Wotton (courtier) and Cuthbert Tunstall (Bishop of Durham).

Thomas Seymour was Baron Seymour of Sudeley and was the younger brother of Edward Seymour, Duke of Somerset and Queen Jane Seymour, Henry VIII's third and favourite wife. Due to their family elevation through the marriage of their sister Jane, the Seymours, who were canny sixteenth century courtiers and politicians, were able to advance themselves during this period of royal favour. Edward Seymour, Duke of Somerset was a great military leader and an ambitious politician. Thomas Seymour, who although ambitious and greedy for power, was more of a peacock courtier. He was a womaniser who made rash judgements, and was more ruled by his passions than his siblings. Henry VIII was able to see this character flaw in him and decided not to include Thomas in Edward's regency council. Henry may also have been punishing Thomas as he had also been a rival for the affections of Katherine Parr, before Henry made her his final wife. Upon King Edward's ascension to the throne, his regency council agreed to ennoble Edward Seymour, bestowing him the title of the Duke of Somerset, and created him Lord Protector for the duration of the new king's minority. Thomas Seymour was jealous of Somerset's influence over their nephew and was possibly encouraged in this sentiment by his new wife Katherine Parr, who had initially thought that she would pay a larger role in her stepson's minority after Henry's death.

During his brief marriage to Katherine Parr, Thomas Seymour struggled to stay out of scandal. His marriage started off in this controversial vein due to the swiftness of his nuptials to the dowager queen Katherine Parr so soon after the death of the late king. The couple soon became expectant parents and during this time, Thomas was implicated in inappropriate behaviour towards the teenage Elizabeth. After Katherine died of childbirth complications, Seymour reset his power-hungry ambitions on Lady Elizabeth. This persistent pursuit of Elizabeth had less to do with any feelings or emotions but Seymour's arrogant presumption that he should have an equal say over his young nephew, King Edward, as his older brother Somerset. He thought that Elizabeth was key to helping him achieve this goal. The Duke of Somerset and the regency council had run out of patience with Thomas Seymour by early 1549 when he was arrested. Elizabeth witnessed her younger brother having to sign a death warrant for a close relative, his uncle, which is something she had to do during her own reign, first with the Duke of Norfolk and then with Mary Queen of Scots. Unlike her younger brother, Elizabeth struggled both times to condemn her family, but she did eventually listen to the counsel of her advisors, who all assured her that such steps were necessary for her own safety as well as national security.

Edward was a child of post-reformation England and had been brought up within a humanist court. He was taught by a prominent reformist and followed a Protestant doctrine. He was far more reformist and radical in his Protestantism than Elizabeth, and while his father Henry may have started the English Reformation, it was Edward, under the guidance of his regency council, who would reform the English church to be more in line with Lutheran ideologies of Protestantism. The Anglican Church under Henry, at the time of his death, was closer in doctrine to the Catholic ideology than any of the continental reformist doctrines. The biggest change English Christians were asked to make was to acknowledge Henry as their representative on earth rather than the pope in Rome.

Edward eliminated many of the papist traditions that still lingered. This included the lighting of candles and the saying of prayers for the souls of the dead, stained glass windows in religious buildings; the use of incense during mass and a rosary while praying. He also eliminated Latin services and the presence of religious icons within church buildings.

During her brother's reign, Protestant Elizabeth was able to practise her faith freely and in line with her conscience, but she would have been aware of the personal clashes between her two half-siblings over their different religious views. This friction was not helped by the fact that there was a very large age difference between the two of them. At the time of their father's death, Mary had been about to turn 31, while Edward was just nine years old. Mary must have felt humiliated, frustrated and embarrassed to find she was being told how to pray by her little step-brother, and it is not surprising then that she would accidentally and unwittingly become the popular figurehead for her fellow oppressed Catholics and traditionalists.

As a devout Catholic, Mary met with Edward to ask to be able to continue to worship within the Catholic tradition, and she left their meeting under the impression that he was happy with her praying in private as her conscience saw fit. Mary also felt that any legislation regarding faith should not be made until Edward was of age and was able to rule on this delicate subject as a God anointed king rather than a minor, under the influence of the predominately reformist regency council.

Subsequently, when Whitsunday 1549 came around and the law changed, Mary did not feel she needed to use the new Common Book of Prayers as she had spoken with Edward. Word got back to the regency council that the king's step-sister was not complying with the law and it was not pleased. Its members composed a strongly worded letter telling her that she must comply with the Uniformity Act. Just like the Prayer Book rebels in the West Country, Mary did not obey and wrote an equally strongly worded missive back to her brother's council. The Lord Protector, The Duke of Somerset, knew that this situation had to be handled carefully as Mary was related to the Holy Roman Emperor, Charles V, and any false move could have sparked an international incident or worse. In the end, Somerset became too distracted by the imminent problem of the Prayer Book Rebellion to worry about how Mary prayed.

Thomas Seymour would not be the last of the young king's maternal family to go the block during his short reign. The same fate awaited his favourite uncle and his Lord Protector, Edward Seymour, Duke of Somerset. Somerset was arrogant and he assumed that because he was the highest noble in the land, as well as being related to the king, this made him not only untouchable but superior, to his peers on the privy council and at court. It was this attitude that led him to the executioner's block, because the higher you rose within any of the Tudor courts, the less advisable it was to make enemies because the further you had to fall. Somerset's arrogance was not the only thing that made him unpopular with his fellow privy counsellors and courtiers. England had at this time been through a rough patch with a new monarch, especially one as young as Edward, the shift in reforming the national faith and the consequential Prayer Book Rebellions had all created social tensions across all classes of Tudor society. If mismanaged and not handled carefully, England and her government faced a potential crisis.

In the previous year, Somerset had taken charge of looking into petty grievances from the commoners. Many of the complaints were aimed at landlords who used the tenants' common land to graze their sheep, cows or ponies. Somerset put a man called John Hales in charge of the investigative commissions. Hales was the honourable member of parliament for Preston in Lancashire and an acting Justice of the Peace for the counties of Warwick and Middlesex, making him an ideal candidate for this role. However, Hales, like the young king, was a reformer and brought his morals and religious zeal with him in his new role within the commission. The outcome of the individual cases mainly favoured the tenants, and as a result, many courtiers, who were also landlords, resented Somerset for making Hales head of the inquiries.

The biggest enemy that the Duke of Somerset made was John Dudley, the Duke of Warwick. Both men served on Edward's privy council however their views clashed and Somerset with his arrogant mindset and senior position failed to pay heed to Warwick's advice. He also failed to listen to the opinions and views of the rest of the privy council as well. One of the areas that Warwick and Somerset clashed on was their views on Scotland. Warwick wanted to remove the soldiers stationed across the northern border as currently there was no unrest in Scotland. Somerset, who was in charge of the men stationed there, argued that the very reason there was peace in the Highlands was because there were English soldiers garrisoned there; the situation was at a frustrating stalemate and the animosity between the rivals deepened. Relations between the two men went beyond being salvaged when Warwick requested that the offices made vacant due to the death of Sir Andrew Flammock be granted to him and his family. Warwick felt that these newly available offices should be bestowed upon his family for his contribution in quashing the riots and unrest caused by the Prayer Book Rebellion. Somerset declined this request to Warwick and whether from greed, spite or to flex his power and prove that he was the more senior of the two men, he rewarded these offices and incomes to Warwick's long-time rival and enemy, Thomas Fisher.

In the autumn of 1549, Somerset, now friendless, having lost the confidence and support of many within the privy council, started to become paranoid, fearing that he was about to lose his grip on power and the control he had over the king. The events of the month of October are conflicted and unclear. It is known that Warwick and his privy council allies, safe in the knowledge that Somerset was away in the country, held a clandestine meeting discussing how to remove the Duke of Somerset from the role of Lord Protectorate - in the vain hope of curbing his paranoid, dangerous and selfish political agenda, which threatened not only the peace of the nation but the king's person. When the business of the state and privy council restarted at the Tudor palace of Hampton Court, the first few days continued as normal until the 4 October when Warwick failed to attend court and council.

Somerset's reaction to Warwick's absence without leave was to summon extra armed men to increase the king's protection at Hampton Court Palace. As much as it would have been for the king's safety, no doubt, Somerset was also thinking of his own protection as well. Somerset knew that as long as he had the king's trust, he would be safe. Sadly, he had not taken note of his brother's error in thinking this same way. Although he was clearly fearful that he and the king were in danger, Somerset had no evidence that there was a legitimate threat to either of them. He needed to address the men who had come to support him and encourage them to stay.

In the end, Somerset was desperate to blame this perceived threat on someone, and so he pronounced that his nephew Edward was under threat from his eldest stepsister, the Catholic Lady Mary. This move was both clever and very dangerous. The men who approached Somerset said they felt that their souls were at risk from Mary and that they feared for the safety of the king if Lady Mary became Edward's regent. Such religious passion could easily have sparked unrest in an already tense City of London, causing discord that could have spread throughout the nation; it was a dangerous gamble.

As Somerset had called men to guard the king and himself, Warwick had also been busy recruiting men to help him fight Somerset. These recruits gathered at Warwick's London residency, Ely Place, located within London's Holborn area, on 6 October, the first Sunday of the month. Warwick convinced his followers that the country was at the point of civil war and that Somerset was to blame for this social and political unrest. He argued that Somerset's arrogance and vanity had resulted in his refusal to listen to the advice of the privy council. They also agreed that they needed the support of the City of London if they were going to be successful in protecting the young king and removing his vain uncle.

On Monday 7 October, the divisions within the privy council were made visible, Warwick had the backing of seventeen of the twenty-five counsellors. Later that day, the influential men of the City of London met at the Guildhall to discuss the growing and troubling political crisis as both Somerset and Warwick had written to the Guildhall. Those at the Guildhall met and examined the situation in a measured and careful fashion and they decided that Somerset was the problem and that they would work with Warwick and his lords to protect the king and their city. However, this decision stopped short of giving Warwick more armed men in order to depose the Lord Protector. The guildsmen and aldermen did as much as they could to support Warwick without crossing the fine line that could be misconstrued as treason should Warwick not succeed in his plan.

Somerset sent loyal men ahead of himself to London with the goal of securing the strategically important Tower of London. Naively, Somerset underestimated Warwick who had already secured the Norman fortress for his fraction. The Tower of London was vital because it was not only a secure prison, but held a fortress with an arsenal of weaponry, was the location of the London Mint, and a royal palace, making it a safe place for King Edward.

On the 8 October, Warwick and his fraction engaged with Londoners informing them how Somerset had abused his position as Lord Protector towards both the nation and the king. This news was greeted cautiously by the population of London and rightly so, it was a dangerous business taking sides in such a political quagmire, if the side you chose to help failed you were at risk of being charged with treason and facing the hangman's noose. Somerset had also been generous to the common people, and they needed more proof of his misconduct before they fell in behind Warwick and his supporters.

With the Tower of London no longer a secure option to keep King Edward safe, Somerset decided the safest place left to them was down the River Thames at Windsor. The castle located in Berkshire is as fortified as the Tower of London even if it was without the mint and huge arsenal of weapons. Windsor had the bonus of being further away from London, making it safer. The following days saw letters exchanged from Westminster and Windsor, with both sides stating that they only had the young king's best interests at heart. More men had taken Warwick's side and were willing to take up arms and fight the Lord Protector. Somerset was forced to evaluate his situation and to try and find a solution where he could survive this crisis both politically and literally. He did not have long though, and by 9 October, Somerset knew he had lost. The best he could now hope for was to try and stay alive. The privy council had written to him advising that he resign from the post of Lord Protectorate and surrender the king to the care of the privy council.

In a desperate letter addressed directly to Warwick, Somerset reminded his foe that they had once been friends and allies and that their animosity sprung from rumours circulated around court by others.

> 'There hath been from your youth and mine so great a friendship and amity betwixt us, as never for my part to no man was greater, now suddenly there should be hatred; and that without just case whatsoever, rumours and bruits, or persuasion of others have moved you to conceive … I never meant worse to you than to myself' *(The Annals of England (1615) P598)*

Unsurprisingly Warwick was unmoved by his foe's desperate attempt at reconciliation and forgiveness.

The crisis found King Edward in a politically uncertain position. The way in which he tried to smooth troubled waters was to write to his privy council, hoping to strike a level and balanced tone showing no favouritism between his council, Warwick or his uncle Somerset. It is likely that 10-year-old Edward was guided and had this letter drafted for him by the Archbishop of Canterbury, Thomas Cramner, who had survived and thrived within the often turbulent Henrician court.

Cranmer, in his position as archbishop, also wrote to the victorious Warwick and the privy council pleading for clemency towards his fellow reformist Somerset as seen in the following extract: 'Life is sweet my lords, and they say you seek his blood and his death… if you have conceived any such determination to put it out of your heads and incline your hearts to kindness and humanity.' *(Tyler I, pp223-7)* Warwick and the council sent a reply on the 10 October, giving Somerset misleading reassurances of clemency for his actions. However the following day, Somerset was arrested, removed from court and was relocated to the thirteenth century Beauchamp Tower, within Windsor Castle's compound, and kept under a secure guard. He held on to the title of Lord Protector for another two days before being transported to London. Officially, the privy council was able to accuse Somerset of twenty separate charges of treason. As Somerset headed to the Tower of London, to await his fate, Edward moved to Hampton Court Palace. On the 15 October, a new privy council had to be appointed and they needed to dissolve the position of Lord Protector. However, on 20 October, Warwick was created the Lord Admiral of the Royal Navy, elevating him significantly in status from his peers on the council. King Edward and his new council remained at Hampton Court until 17 October when they made a grand entrance into London. Thousands of people come to see their king as the disgraced duke grew accustomed to the Tower of London.

The fallen Duke of Somerset found himself subject to daily interviews in relation to the charges that had been brought against him. Even when he had been brought low and at great risk of losing both his freedom and life, Somerset remained arrogant, refusing to answer the questions posed to him by his captors. He spent Christmas in The Tower but was eventually released on 6 Febraury 1550. During the spring of 1550, Somerset was able to regain admission to the royal court and was even invited back to the privy council on 11 May, barely three months after being released from the Tower of London, having escaped charges of treason. His experience had done little to change his attitude or behaviour and had merely brought himself a couple of years reprieve. Somerset's relationship with Warwick never changed as the two men were never able to put aside their petty rivalry for the young king's approval and their own power-hungry greed. The two rivals, Somerset and Warwick, attempted to work together within the privy council until October 1551, when Warwick aided by the Duke of Northumberland had enough evidence to reorder Somerset's arrest. The king's disgraced uncle learnt his fate when his trial concluded on 1 December 1551 and he was inevitably found guilty by his peers.

In order to remove any blame or guilt for executing the king's favourite uncle, the privy council passed a swift change of law stating that once the king had signed a document, it no longer required six signatures from his council to ratify it in law as the king was the highest authority in the land making any other signatures were surplus to requirement. The privy council had not only managed to remove Somerset but also ensured that they avoided retribution and blame if the young king regretted the execution later. Many historians believe that the king was encouraged by William Paulet, the Marquis of Winchester, to bring the matter of his uncle's fate to the top of the agenda in early 1552. The longer Somerset was imprisoned in The Tower, the greater the chance he had of pardon from his nephew, and so the council needed to move swiftly. Somerset's death warrant was drawn up on the 19 January 1552. It was only then that Warwick had finally won in this political battle as the second of the young king's uncles was sent to the executioner.

Edward Seymour, late Earl of Somerset, former Lord Protectorate and uncle to the king, went to Tower Hill on 22 January 1552. He died bravely like the military man that he was and after praying he addressed the small crowd who had gathered to watch him meet his maker. Even in his last words upon earth, Edward Seymour remained arrogantly stubborn:

> '…I have to say to you concerning religion: I have always, being in authority, a furtherer of it to the glory of God to the uttermost of my power; whereof I am nothing sorry, but rather have cause and do rejoice most gladly that I have done, for the mightiest benefit of God that ever I had, or any man might have in this world.' *(BL Cotton Charter iv,17)*

Elizabeth had witnessed the complex politics of her younger brother's court. She had seen how two of his maternal uncles both went to the scaffold for their arrogance and greed. She must have questioned Edward's reasoning. However later, she too would understand when she was faced with her own hard decisions on whether to execute her relatives the Duke of Norfolk and Mary Queen of Scots. But as Warwick and the privy council settled into governing without the threat or influence of the late Duke of Somerset, the young king's future was about to be threatened by a different enemy – illness.

In the late spring of 1553, Edward contracted both measles and smallpox. Measles, although serious, is today treatable as well as highly preventable through immunisation. Smallpox on the other hand, was truly deadly disease. Fatalities from smallpox were high, and those who did survive often were left with disfiguring scars and even blindness. Edward battled both contagious diseases and miraculously survived. Correspondence from the young king, can be found dated 12 April within the calendar of state papers.

Elizabeth replied the following to her stepbrother when she heard that he had recovered from his illness; '[Smallpox] is to be countered no sickness that shall cause a better health when it is past than was assured afore it came.' *(Elizabeth, Complete works: Letters pp.36-7)*

Unfortunately for Edward that was not to be the case as smallpox had in fact weakened his immune system and made it harder for him to fight the tuberculosis that would kill him within the year. After recovering, the young king now aged 14, started to take a more active role in the governing of his kingdom with the aid and guidance of his privy council. By October 1552, it became apparent to the court and the privy council that the king was growing sickly. The counsellors were so worried about Edward that they appointed a leading sixteenth century Italian doctor Hieronymus Cardano, to examine the king in the hope that he would be able to diagnose what was ailing him. After making his examination, Cardano concluded that Edward was of good intelligence, unsurprisingly he presented himself as older than his years in maturity, was slightly hard of hearing and required the aid of glasses and a magnifying glass to help him read. The need for glasses is not surprising as his father, Henry VIII, also required help from reading glasses. Cardano proceeded to give Edward a clean bill of health. Sadly, his assessment was incorrect.

The festive period in Edward's court came and went and slowly the king grew frailer and weaker, so much so, that when his eldest stepsister

Lady Mary came to visit him in January 1553, she found her young brother in bed with a cough. As January passed into February and then into March, the king failed to show signs of improvement. On 1 March the State Opening of Parliament was relocated to the Palace of Whitehall due to the king's poor health. To give perspective on how ill Edward was the Palace of Whitehall was located a short walk down the road from Westminster Hall.

As the weather warmed, his royal household hoped that the spring air would help ease the king's condition and Edward was put through a regime of light exercise and was relocated to Greenwich Palace east of London, for cleaner air. Still he grew frailer, and he had now started coughing up blood. Consumption, today better known as tuberculosis, and often shortened to TB, had made its way into the king's respiratory system and his compromised and weakened immune system could no longer fight the disease attacking his lungs. The move to Greenwich had only temporarily eased Edward's symptoms, and by 12 May 1553, he was gravely ill again. It was during this last few weeks of his life, that Edward drew up the infamous *Device for the Succession of the Crown* that would name his cousin, Lady Jane Grey as his successor instead of his elder stepsister Lady Mary. Below is a transcription of the Device for Succession of the Crown in its original English written by the dying Edward and probably composed with the help of Warwick and the privy council.

My devise for the Succession

1. For lakke of issu *[masle inserted above the line, but afterwards crossed out]* of my body *[to the issu (masle above the line) cumming of thissu femal, as i have after declared inserted, but crossed out]*. To the L Franceses heires masles, *[For lakke of erased] [if she have any inserted]* such issu *[befor my death inserted]* to the L' Janes *[and her]* heires masles, To the L Katerins heires masles, To the L Maries heires masles, To the heires masles of the daughters wich she shal haue hereafter. Then to the L Margets heires masles. For lakke of such issu, To th'eires masles of the L Janes daughters. To th'eires masles of the L Katerins daughters, and so forth til yow come to the L Margets *[daughters inserted]* heires masles.
2. If after my death theire masle be entred into 18 yere old, then he to have the hole rule and gouernauce therof.

3. But if he be under 18, then his mother to be gouuernres til he entre 18 yere old, But to doe nothing w'out th'auise (and agremet inserted) of 6 parcel of a counsel to be pointed by my last will to the nombre of 20.

4. If the mother die befor th'eire entre into 18 the realme to be gouuerned by the cousel Prouided that after he be 14 yere al great matters of importaunce be opened to him.

5. If i died w'out issu, and there were none masle, then the L Fraunces to be (reget altered to) gouuernres. For lakke of her, the her eldest daughters,4 and for lakke of them the L Marget to be gouuernres after as is aforsaid, til sume heire masle be borne, and then the mother of that child to be gouernres.

6. And if during the rule of the gouernres ther die 4 of the counsel, then shal she by her letters cal an assebe of the counsel w'in on month folowing and chose 4 more, wherin she shal haue thre uoices. But after her death the 16 shal chose emong themselfes til th'eire come to (18 erased) 14 yeare olde, and then he by ther aduice shal chose them" (1553).

—Edward VI, Devise for the Succession
(Literary Remains of King Edward the Sixth.. Vol II.
John Gough Nichols, Ed. London: J. B. Nichols and Sons,
for the Roxburghe Club, 1857. Pages 571-2)

The reason Edward's Device for Succession of the Crown was so controversial was because it went against the wishes of his late father, Henry VIII, as set out in his last will and testimony. Henry stated that should Edward die without issue, the throne was to pass to his eldest daughter by Katherine of Aragon, Mary. Henry went further by stating that should Mary also die without producing a Tudor heir, the crown should then pass to his youngest daughter by Anne Boleyn, Lady Elizabeth. Edward did not wish to do this, primarily because Mary had refused to give up her Catholic faith. He could have skipped over Mary on the grounds of faith and made Elizabeth his successor but he possibly feared the consequences of favouring one sister over the other, and so instead, he decided to look to another branch of the family to pass the throne to and carry on the Protestant reforms that he had started.

Initially, Edward did not name Lady Jane Grey, a childhood friend, as his heir, instead passing the throne to any male heirs she would go on to have. Although married at the end of Edward's life, Jane and her husband, Guildford Dudley, had only been married a few months and any new male heirs had yet to be born. The Device for Succession of the Crown was altered days before Edward's death with two little words that would change Jane's fate from mother of the new King to the new monarch instead. These two words changed English history creating Jane the first Queen of England as well as changing her future.

Edward VI, the last Tudor male monarch, finally became consumed by his tuberculosis on Thursday 6 July 1553. Through his death, the fates and fortunes of two women would be changed, as the men around them used them to further their own power and greed in the name of religious reform and unity. What was to come was one of the biggest patriarchal abuses of power recorded in history.

The impact of her younger step-brother's brush with death must have haunted the young Queen Elizabeth when she too contracted smallpox in the early part of her reign in October 1562. It could also be argued that Edward's handling of his succession the following year, when he was gravely ill had a great influence on Elizabeth's views on the subject of her own succession. Elizabeth always refused to name an heir for the English throne in order to prevent plotting by the other possible heirs.

1553: The Nine Day Queen

Lady Jane Grey was the eldest daughter of Henry Grey, the Duke of Suffolk, and was cousin to the royal children as she descended from Henry VIII. She had been educated with Lady Elizabeth within the Parr/Seymour household as Seymour's legal ward and remained there until Katherine died and Seymour was disgraced. Katherine Parr may have been an important influence on the young and impressionable Jane, as she was a strong, assertive woman, something that was a trademark of Jane's short reign, and was also evident in Elizabeth's own more successful occupation of the throne. As well as learning from Katherine, Jane had benefited from a humanist education that was normally only granted to sixteenth century boys. Amongst the subjects she would have learnt from her Protestant tutors were Latin, Greek, Hebrew, Italian and the art of rhetoric. These opportunities were due to the reformation and Protestantism which in many respects had already made her the ideal future of Protestantism within England.

Upon the death of the childless King Edward VI, the *Device for the Succession*, created in the last dying months of his reign, was set in motion by the privy council. Through his Device for the Succession, Edward had firstly disinherited his two stepsisters, and having examined his family tree, had chosen for the throne to now pass through the Grey line who had descended from Henry VII's youngest daughter Mary. Mary Tudor had two daughters, Frances and Eleanor, and Edward had chosen the daughters of Frances to continue the Tudor line, via Frances's eldest daughter, Lady Jane Grey.

At the time of Edward's death, Frances was still alive, yet Edward chose to skip over her and pass his crown to her eldest daughter Jane instead. This may have been because Lady Jane was younger and more likely to produce a male heir. The other possibility may have been that the men in power saw crowning Lady Jane Grey as an opportunity to easily manipulate a young, inexperienced teenager to do their will. Whether intentional or not, Jane did become a pawn to be used by her greedy Tudor family, to gain power and position within the power vacuum created after Edward's death. Sadly, Jane would go on to pay a very heavy personal price for her obedience to these power-greedy men which included her own father.

Edward's death was not immediately shared with the English populous, thus enabling the privy council to start putting his plans into place. There is no way of knowing if the device for the inheritance of the royal throne was solely Edward's idea or whether he was encouraged or coaxed into drawing it up by his regency council. But given that Warwick, now the Duke of Northumberland, was Edward's chief minister, he did have a vested interest in Jane becoming the next English monarch, making it less than likely to have been only Edward's idea. This is strengthened further when you know that Northumberland and Jane's father, Henry Grey were close colleagues and conspirators on the privy council. The Duke of Northumberland's son Guildford was engaged to be married to the eldest Grey daughter and new heir to the throne, Lady Jane. The couple married on 25 May 1553 at Durham House, owned by the Duke of Northumberland. The home was located on the bank of the River Thames at what is today the site of the Victoria Embankment Gardens. Edward was by that date already in his sickbed fighting the tuberculosis that would eventually kill him, but he welcomed the news of the wedding with a royal warrant and gift of clothes for the wedding party.

After Edward's death, the first thing that the Duke of Northumberland needed to do was to keep Lady Mary from taking the throne that was rightfully hers according to her father's will. Henry VIII had named her as the second in line to the throne, should Edward die childless. This was regardless of the fact that she was a woman, a Catholic, and technically still illegitimate by law. The reason Henry agreed to this was probably because he never imagined that such circumstances would ever arise to allow either of his daughters to take the throne.

As her brother, the king, lay dying in his bed, Mary had been forewarned that the Duke of Northumberland would likely use this opportunity to imprison her or worse kill her so that she could not take the throne upon Edward's death. Sensibly, Mary decided to put as much distance between Greenwich and herself as well as making a list of trusted friends and allies she could rely on in the coming days and weeks.

The first thing that Northumberland needed to do was to take control of the Tower of London. He had to be prepared incase Mary fought for her birthright. To ensure that they had a chance of keeping Jane on the throne, it was vital that Northumberland and the privy council take control of the fortress as well as The Tower's armoury. Two days after his death, the population of London and England were still unaware that Edward had died and that England had a new Queen; but who would she be, Lady Jane Grey or Lady Mary Tudor?

On 9 July 1553, Jane was told by her new father-in-law, the Duke of Northumberland, that she and not Mary, was the new Queen of England. It is important to remember that Jane was just 15-years-old. This shocking news was encouraged by her parents, possibly accompanied by threats until Jane finally accepted the role that made her the new Protestant Queen of England. Jane as a mature, well-educated girl must have realised the gravity and potential danger she was now in, especially if Mary issued an alternative claim for the throne.

As Jane was being told she was the new queen, Mary was starting her counterattack from her estates based in Norfolk. She started writing to local prominent landowners asking for support to protect her and the country through raising armed men. All of her letters were signed off as 'Mary, the Queene'.

On Monday 10 July 1553, Jane was publicly declared as the new Queen of England. Her first public appearance happened on a barge ride from Northumberland's home, Syon House, to the Tower of London. Little did Jane know that she would never leave the Tower of London again. The power and influence of the Duke of Northumberland was noticeable when the royal party arrived at the Tower of London. Although Jane was proclaimed queen it was Northumberland's son Guildford who stood in a symbolically prominent position ahead of Jane, publicly declaring that Northumberland assumed that Guildford would be England's new king in equal status to his wife, Jane. This is reflected in letters sent to France from the French ambassador who mentions 'Le nouveau Roi' - the new king - rather than the new queen. The Venetian ambassador also passed comment on Guildford's position within the welcome party in his correspondence back to the Venetian Republic's Doge.

Before long, rumours had started to spread around London and beyond that the Duke of Northumberland had poisoned the late king in order to put Jane and his son on the throne. Unfortunately, Northumberland had become a disliked public figure within the country before putting Jane and Guildford in their new positions. This new action caused further disdain amongst the commoners towards Northumberland. One of the main reasons he was so disliked was that he had been prominent in quashing the popular revolts of 1549, which required the use of foreign professional soldiers against Englishmen.

In a bid to convince the populace of London and the rest of the country that Jane was the rightful new queen, the privy council had a royal proclamation of Jane's succession declared, explaining how she was had been made queen instead of Mary. The royal proclamation was printed and distributed throughout the land - this was the first time in history that it was necessary for those in power to explain how a monarch was justified to take the crown. This was done with the city heralds loudly pronouncing the complexities of how Jane became queen.

Also, on 10 July, Mary made her first move against the Grey reign. She sent a letter to the privy council in the Tower of London, saying that as a gesture of goodwill, if they abandoned Jane and supported her rightful claim to the throne, she would ensure that no personal repercussions or consequences would befall them for their misjudgment. Mary also outlined in her letter that if they failed to change sides, she would do all she could to get the throne, even if that meant starting a civil war. The gauntlet had been thrown and the battle of wills had begun.

Not surprisingly, none of Jane's privy council accepted Mary's offer of pardon and instead responded to her letter and its threats by sending out letters to all the gentry they believed to be in favour of Jane's claim to the crown, asking for support against Mary's 'untrue claim'. In order to make these letters official, her privy council persuaded Jane to officially sign their correspondence as 'Jane the Queene'. One sign that people were unconvinced of Jane's claim was that Northumberland had to offer twice the normal daily rate to get men in London to form an army to defend the new queen's claim. This was in an age before England had a standing national army and national defence was made up of local militia comprising of apprentices and able-bodied men, who were required by law to undertake regular archery practice.

The Duke of Northumberland, Henry Grey and even Guildford Dudley had all up to this point underestimated Jane's character and the strength of her personality, having assumed that she would naturally be obediently submissive and a puppet easy to control and manipulate due to her being of the 'weaker sex'. But Jane was a child of the Protestant reformation and was descended from a long line of assertive and strong Tudor women. Why would she have been any different from these strong assertive women? Jane's first action was to declare that Guildford would be made a duke but not pronounced king. For many historians of this period, it is widely believed that this was the turning point when Jane had had enough of being used by the powerful men of her family who had thrust her into this position. Her actions from this point show that she was determined to assert herself and make the best of a situation she had not asked for or wanted.

By 12 July, Mary had managed to generate enough support, enabling her to move from her modest manner of Kenning Hall in Norfolk to Framlingham Castle in Suffolk which was also part of her inherited estates. It is important to note that many of the men who were coming to her aid were her tenants from her estates and unlike Northumberland and Jane, she did not bribe her support with high wages. These men flocked to Mary out of loyalty to their landlord. They also felt that she was the rightful successor to the crown. Another point to make is that Catholics would naturally migrate to Mary and support her, but many Protestants also joined her swelling army of supporters. Mary was very clever in making her headquarters in East Anglia as the Duke of Northumberland was still deeply resented there. He had been vicious in his actions during the popular revolt of 1549 led by Robert Kett. Many of the locals would have lost fathers, sons, brothers and uncles at Northumberland's hands four years earlier. And it was too soon for the locals to forgive Northumberland or support his power games and 'puppet' queen. When Mary arrived at the Norman fortress of Framlingham, she was greeted with lots of local support. She may have been the underdog away from London, but Mary had the peoples' backing. She was also Henry VIII's daughter.

Jane's side was also rallying together at the Tower of London. Northumberland's biggest mistake at this crucial time was underestimating Mary level of support. She came to from a long line of strong, fighting, Catholic monarchs. Her grandparents had been Isabella and Ferdinand, who defeated and eradicated the Islamic Moors out of southern Spain and her mother, was Katherine of Aragon, who had dared to fight Henry tooth and nail when he requested a divorce from her in favour of Anne Boleyn; it was a therefore arrogant to have underestimated Mary.

The new Queen and her council were starting to struggle and they had made a terrible mistake, deciding that Jane's father, Henry Grey, who was little more than a bumbling administrator, with no war or leadership experience, should be the person to meet Mary's troops. They did not expect Mary's army to be as strong or as well-armed as their own side. Jane decided to exercise her power and vetoed the council's decision sending the hated Northumberland to face Mary's troops instead. Jane had unwittingly helped Mary, first by sending Northumberland into territory that despised him and also, by sending the duke away, she had weakening her position in London as he had been the mastermind of the plan to make her queen in the first place. This left Jane vulnerable and a privy council without a confident leader. All it could take is a disagreement and things could easily go wrong in his absence. It was a fatal judgement of error.

As the 13 July dawned, Mary was in the strongest position she had been in since the death of her brother, Edward. Jane had sent her most able politician to fight. Prior to leaving, Northumberland reminded the privy counsellors that they had all freely sworn allegiance to Jane and that this was where their loyalty lay. The start of the doubt and political fractures had started to appear within Jane's camp. The members of the privy council were not the only men who were starting to have doubts. During the course of a day, the gentry within the rest of the country started to change its allegiance towards Mary. The gentry needed the support of their tenants in times of crisis, so as their people chose to support Mary so did their over lords. One of the lords to have listened to his tenants' will and who was forced to defect to Mary was the Earl of Oxford. He was given an ultimatum, either declare for Mary or they would join Mary in defiance of their landlord; Oxford followed the will of his men and Mary gained another lord. Another reason why Mary was able to attract and charm the populous was because unlike Jane, Mary was visible to the people who supported her while Jane was locked away, hiding within the safety of the Tower of London. This was a powerful and courageous strategy on Mary's part.

The very next day on the 14 July, the remaining members of the privy council with Jane in The Tower started to crumble and divide. Even though some of the counsellors still supported Northumberland through and through, others in his absence, had now began to feel less reassured in what they were doing while others did not like the fact that a

15-year-old girl was asserting herself over them - despite them being the ones who had elevated her to the higher status of monarch. Their division made Jane extremely vulnerable. With little to do while Northumberland was fighting for her, Jane looked to keeping herself busy by evaluating the content of the royal wardrobe. By comparison, her rival Mary, was rallying all the people who had gathered to support her.

By the sixth day of Jane's ill-fated reign, Northumberland was still on his way to take on Mary. His military plan was to surround Mary with his armed men. Northumberland had even taken into consideration the fact that Mary was located close to the coast and placed six ships offshore in case Mary attempted to escape to her maternal family in Europe. The ships were fully armed with men and weaponry from the Tower of London. Northumberland had however made a mistake as he had failed to pay the soldiers and crew of these ships. An enterprising young supporter and member of Mary's household, Henry Jerningham overheard the frustrating predicament of the unhappy crew and he decided to turn this to Mary's advantage. As luck would have it, the ships had been forced to come in and take shelter upon the Orwell Estuary due to dangerous conditions in the North Sea. Jerningham took it upon himself to make his way to the docked ships and managed to speak with the captains of the vessels. He was able to persuade them to abandon Jane in favour of Mary who now had access to gun power and control of the coast as well as trained men; all due to Jerningham's initiative. News of this mutiny reached the ears of the privy council on the 16 July. The effects of this news only increased the fear and doubt that had taken hold amongst the counsellors. It was now dawning on them that they may lose this fight and probably their lives too. They had assumed that the fighting would take place away from London, but they soon learnt that some of Mary's supporters from the counties of Oxfordshire and Buckinghamshire were planning to try and take London for Mary. The fortification of the Tower of London was put into lockdown and guards increased within the barricades - The Tower had now effectively turned from royal palace to prison for Jane. As well as these additional defences at The Tower, many of the gates of London were also locked and guarded by armed men in the hopes of protecting the City of London.

By the 17 July 1553, the crisis was nearing its political and religious climax. Jane had been de facto queen for eight days, but as time moved on, the chances of her holding onto the title of queen were looking less and less likely, unlike Mary, whose support kept growing. Northumberland had made it to Cambridgeshire, and his military plan was still to capture - not kill - Mary so that she could not threaten Jane's reign. He had wanted to attack Mary at the Framlingham property but was delayed for two days in the university town while he waited for additional men and weapons to arrive prior to the attack. The delay was a big mistake as Mary had not been resting upon her laurels, her support had grown, and the duke was still unaware that his naval ships had mutinied and changed alliance.

On the ninth and final day of Jane's reign, Northumberland started to advance towards Mary, and Jane's privy council received worrying reports and rumours that one of their members, Sir Edmund Peckham, who had held the position of the Treasurer of the Royal Mint, had escaped and defected to Mary. This was a big loss for Jane's side, not only had Peckham changed sides but he had also rallied men from the home counties of Berkshire, Oxfordshire, Buckinghamshire and Middlesex who were armed and approaching London to take the city for Mary. This seems to have been the point when the last of the doubters amongst her council decided that they should abandon Jane. Like rats on a sinking ship, the privy counsellors started to flee The Tower, including Jane's own uncle, the Earl of Arundel. As the council abandoned Jane, Northumberland received the news that Mary had gathered support that outnumbering his men three to one and that his naval defences had defected; he too decided not to carry on and confront Mary. Instead Northumberland retreated back to Cambridge to consider his next move.

There was no confrontation and by the end of the 18 July, Mary had all but won the crisis without having to even go into battle. Jane was now virtually alone in The Tower with just her father, Sir Henry Grey and her husband Guildford Dudley remaining loyal to her. Down the river at Durham House, Jane's former privy council had met, so that they could try and find a way to save their heads from the block. They decided to shift the blame to Northumberland and declare for Mary. Their last act as a council was to send a message to the Tower of London informing Jane that she was no longer Queen of England. The difficult task of breaking the bad news fell to her overly ambitious father, Sir Henry Grey. When he located his daughter, to deliver the message, he found her sitting under a cloth of the state, which he proceeded to remove before telling her that Mary had won. It is traditionally thought that Jane had naively asked if she could now go home. If this is true, it is a poignant reminder of just how young and naive she was, thinking she could just walk away from actively engaging in high treason.

In mere moments, Jane went from queen to prisoner when guards from The Tower entered the state room and arrested both herself and her father. Jane was brought out of the royal apartments to a small house just off Tower Green. This house was the home of Mr Nathaniel Partridge and she was once again a commoner, known simply as Lady Jane Dudley.

Mary had now been proclaimed queen in London and the city cheered for the first time since the crisis began. When the Duke of Northumberland heard of Mary's triumph, he tried in a last ditched attempt to reconcile with Mary by proclaiming her queen within Cambridge. But even he must have known that he had gone too far and would pay the ultimate price for his part in this disastrous scheme. It had been an enormous gamble, but he had lost and was now nothing but a traitor.

Elizabeth would have witnessed the rise and fall of her cousin Jane and the triumph of her half-sister Mary. She would have seen the way in which men manipulated and used her cousin for their own greedy gain and ambition. This may have been another event that helped Elizabeth's conscience to justify never wanting to marry. Although Queen Mary had shown their cousin Jane mercy and had tried to spare her life, she did eventually execute her as she had become a dangerous figurehead for the Protestants of England. This too may have influenced Elizabeth's reluctance and delaying tactics in signing Mary Queen of Scot's death warrant, over three decades later. Lastly, Elizabeth also would have learnt that the populace of England had loved her father and as his daughter, Mary was assumed and expected to have been queen upon Edward's death. This must have given Elizabeth hope should Mary die heirless, that the populous would have a similar feelings of expectation and welcome towards her as she too was the daughter of the great King Henry VIII.

1554: The Wyatt Rebellion

Between the death of Edward VI and the coronation of Mary Tudor, England had experienced the failed reign of Lady Jane Grey and had undergone yet another change in religious denomination. Edward had in his short reign strengthened and radicalised English Protestantism, changing the new Anglican church to make it more akin to continental doctrines of Protestantism such as Lutherism or Calvinism. When Protestant Jane lost the throne, Mary brought back Catholicism to England. Coming from Spanish ancestry through her mother, Katherine of Aragon, Mary had never wavered in her Catholic faith, and her close links to Spain made many Protestants fear that the new queen may introduce something similar to the Spanish Inquisition in England. These fears increased when Mary refused to marry an English husband and instead opted to marry Philip II of Spain. She chose him because he was both her equal as a monarch, Catholic in faith, and he strengthened her links to her mother's homeland of Spain.

The Wyatt Rebellion was orchestrated by Sir Thomas Wyatt, Sir James Croft, Sir Peter Carew MP and the Duke of Suffolk, Henry Grey. They had hoped to set off four separate uprisings and to bring their followers to London to depose but not assassinate Mary and put Elizabeth - not Lady Jane Grey - on the throne in order to keep the Spanish rule and a potential Catholic line of succession away from the English monarchy. Wyatt, Croft, Carew and Suffolk were all Protestant in faith.

Although it was a Protestant rebellion, the plotters hoped that the French would help them achieve their aims as France and Spain were big rivals. The French role in the rebellion would be to help the English block the channel from the Spanish so Philip II could not land. Indeed, the French ambassador to England at the time, Antoine de Noailles, would become embroiled in these half-baked plans. It is worth noting that although these events did impact on Elizabeth during the rest of her sister's reign, it was in fact Lady Jane Grey who would pay the ultimate price for the actions carried out by Wyatt and her father the Duke of Suffolk.

The plans were not supposed to start until early spring however when details of the rebellion were leaked to Bishop Stephen Gardiner, they subsequently became known within Mary's court by her privy council. There were only two options open to the plotters: abandon plans or start immediately. Foolishly, they decided to do the latter and executed their plans before they were ready, to disastrous and deadly consequences.

The first person arrested in association with the plot was Edward Courtney, 1st Earl of Devon who was seized and questioned on 21 January 1554. Sir James Croft was slightly wiser and realising that this premature attempt at rebellion was doomed to fail, stopped putting the plan into action. West Country MP Sir Peter Carew attempted to whip up support within his constituency. His constituents were weary of joining him, having so recently felt rough justice after the Prayer Book Revolt of 1549. This part of the West Country was also largely Catholic, so they were even more unwilling to join their MP and the rebels.

Lady Jane Grey's father, the Duke of Suffolk, was the most persistent of the group of plotters (believing that Elizabeth might be a more submissive ruler than his willful daughter.) He was the most determined to carry out this daring plan and was able to attract a small group of men willing to join with him; but the number of followers willing to take part was still under two hundred men. Wyatt was charismatic enough to attract bigger numbers of support for the rebellion that would go on to take his name. Although the rebels were defeated in Rochester, they grew in numbers within the county of Kent. This was probably due to the fact that Kent was a largely Protestant area within the south of England.

Mary's troops were led by 81-year-old Thomas Howard, the Duke of Norfolk. Unfortunately, large numbers of the queen's men defected to the rebels, causing Norfolk to retreat back to London, having failed to put down the rebellion. Worryingly for Mary, the rebels led by Wyatt were able to get as far as Southwark by early February. However London was able to hold them back and Mary's side took control of London Bridge. Mary also had the advantage of having further armed men at her disposal, based within the Tower of London, and located not far away. Wyatt did not surrender despite his weaker position, and instead led his rebels onwards until they were finally stopped near Ludgate and St Paul's.

Around ninety men were executed for joining the rebel lords in their failed plot, including Wyatt himself. He surrendered himself up after he was defeated at Ludgate and was subsequently sent to trial. After his arrest, Wyatt was interrogated and tortured in the hope that he would provide damning evidence against Elizabeth. Even under the pain of torture, Wyatt protected Elizabeth. Naturally, he was found guilty of high treason and endured a traitor's death. He was executed as a traitor on 11 April 1554 when he was hung and drawn from the noose before death and quartered so that his body could be tarred and displayed as a warning to the rest of London. Right until his death, Wyatt proclaimed Elizabeth's innocence.

The Grey family was most affected as a consequence of the rebellion. The Duke of Suffolk, who had taken a very active part in the uprising, along with his brother Thomas Grey were both tried and found guilty. As members of the gentry, they were beheaded. But the saddest pair to die as a direct result of this uprising did not even take part in the revolt and had been held at the Tower of London during the whole time; they were Lady Jane Grey and her husband Lord Guildford Dudley. Jane had not even been the one intended to take the throne had the rebellion been successful. She had been living with a death sentence over her head since the previous November when she had been found guilty of high treason for her nine-day reign. Jane had been sentenced to death by either burning at the stake or beheading within the Tower of London at the queen's pleasure; but her sentence had not until now been carried out. After the events of the Wyatt Rebellion and the guilt of her father and uncle, both Jane and Guildford were on borrowed time. Mary knew that it was dangerous to keep Jane alive any longer for she could attract more plots in the future. And consequently, Mary made February a busy month at the Tower for the Grey family.

On 12 February 1554, Jane's husband was brought to Tower Hill where he was beheaded as a traitor in public. Cruelly, the remains of Guildford were brought back in sight of Jane's window. Thankfully, she had no time left to dwell on that last distressing sight of her husband, as she was shortly led out to Tower Green, located within the confines of the Tower of London. She was taken to a scaffold, accompanied by her maid servant. Upon the scaffold, she made a short address to the small crowd gathered to watch her die. Jane was no more than 17 at the time of her death, and was an extraordinary young woman, for she then recited

Psalm 51 in English - most likely to have been from the Coverdale's translation of the psalm. Below are the first four verses of the Coverdale translation of the psalm into sixteenth century English:

'Haue mercy vpon me (o God) after thy goodnes, and acordinge vnto thy greate mercies, do awaye myne offences. Wash me well from my wickednesse, and clense me fro my synne. For I knowlege my fates, and my synne is euer before me. Agaynst the only, haue I synned, and done euell in thy sight: that thou mightest be iustified in thy saynges, and shuldest ouercome when thou art iudged.' (Coverdales bible psalm 51: verses 1-4)

Her maid's last duty was to take Jane's gloves and handkerchief from her mistress. As per tradition, the executioner asked Jane to forgive him for what he was about to do and then she tied her blindfold around her head. Unable to see, Jane momentarily panicked when she could not find the block to place her head and was helped by one of the lieutenants of The Tower, who was there to witness her death. Jane's last words were a quote from the gospel of Luke 'Lord into thy hands I commend my spirit' and with that, the executioner did his work. Her father, the Duke of Suffolk met the same fate on Tower Hill eleven days after his daughter went so bravely to her death all because he and several other powerful men felt Mary Tudor was not a suitable queen.

With no evidence or confessions incriminating Elizabeth, Mary was unable to convict and dispose of her younger sister, who she had always disliked. As a precaution, Mary decided to keep Elizabeth under arrest. While rebels attempted to get to London and take Mary, the privy council took no chances and requested that Elizabeth come to court. For Elizabeth, this was one of the most trying periods of her life and she must have known that she was stepping dangerously close to the same fate as her mother. Not surprisingly, Elizabeth was terrified of walking into her sister's court and so replied to the request saying that she was too unwell to travel.

This did not impress Mary. In order to ascertain if her younger half-sister was indeed ill; Mary sent a couple of her own doctors to examine Elizabeth and to report back. The physicians confirmed in their report back to Mary, that Elizabeth was unwell but not so sick that she couldn't undertake the journey to court. Mary's answer was to send a litter and members of her privy council to bring her step-sister to court at Whitehall. Elizabeth was right to have feared her reception at court. No sooner had she arrived she was interrogated by Mary's chief minister - Stephen Gardiner, the Bishop of Winchester who was not known for his gentle manners in the interview room. Elizabeth remained calm and kept reiterating that she had nothing to do with the failed Wyatt plot. Requests to see her sister, the queen, were repeatedly denied but eventually Gardiner allowed an isolated and friendless Elizabeth to write to her sister, Mary.

As questioning had not worked, Gardiner and Mary's next tactic was to move Elizabeth to the infamous Tower of London in the hope that it would scare her into telling them what they needed to convict her of treason. Elizabeth was transported to the formidable fortress by boat up the River Thames from Whitehall on 17 March 1554 and was brought into the prison via the feared Traitor's Gate water entrance. Before being moved to the Tower, Elizabeth wrote one of the most important letters of her life to date. It was to her sister Mary:

> 'I am by your Counsel from you commanded to go unto the tower a place more wonted for a false traitor, than a true subject wiche thoghth I knowe I deserve it not, yet in the face of al this realme aperes that it is provid…And therefor I humbly beseche your majestie to let me answer afore your selfe and not suffer me to trust your counselors yea and that afore i go to the tower (if it be possible) if not afor I be further condemned' *(The tide letter - National Archieves Kew 17 March 1554, (Sp 11/4/2 f.3-3v))*

At the end of the letter, Elizabeth drew lines to stop anyone adding any incriminating postscripts to her letter. History shows us that if Mary had received the letter, she did not grant her sister any of her requests.

Elizabeth was held within the apartments of the Bell Tower. Although she was imprisoned, she was in relative comfort but was soon restricted from taking exercise when Mary's council heard that she was mixing with the warden's children on the castle walls. There was some comfort for Elizabeth during these trying months within The Tower; Robert Dudley was also being held prisoner within The Tower at the same time. Dudley's cell was situated in the Beauchamp Tower and he had been in residence there since the fall of Lady Jane Grey. During that time, he had seen both his father, John Dudley and his brother Guildford Dudley, husband to Lady Jane Grey, go to their deaths up on Tower Hill. Dudley had faced trial himself at the end of 1553 and had pleaded guilty to his charges of treason, he was in The Tower at this time waiting for his death sentence to be carried out. He would eventually be pardoned by Mary in early 1555.

After sixty-three days held in custody within the Tower of London, Elizabeth was finally released on 19 May 1554, to be placed under house arrest at Woodstock Manor in Oxfordshire. It is widely believed that Elizabeth was freed from The Tower due to a request from Mary's controversial soon-to-be husband Philip II of Spain. His motivations were purely political. He knew that if anything happened to Elizabeth, regardless of his new wife's personal feelings towards her sibling, it would be politically dangerous for them both because Elizabeth was popular and well loved by the people. If she had succumbed to poison or Mary had executed her, Philip knew that the people of England would blame him and his Spanish Catholic influence upon the queen rather than Mary herself, thus making him even more unpopular. He knew that it was politically more sensible to remove her from The Tower and keep a very close eye on her. There is an irony to the fact that it was Philip who helped Elizabeth during this terrible period of her life during Mary's reign and that later, he would try to invade England and kill Elizabeth during her own incumbency of the throne.

Elizabeth's journey from the Tower of London to Oxfordshire took four days on the road and she was chaperoned by a convoy of a hundred guards to ensure her safe arrival. Amongst her entourage was her new goaler, Sir Henry Beddingfield and the party stopped at both Richmond Palace and Windsor Castle on the way to Woodstock. Release from the Tower did not stop Elizabeth fearing for her life, and over the coming weeks her anxiety and fear made her unwell. Elizabeth's new prison was far more comfortable than The Tower had been, she was treated more like a highly supervised house guest rather than a suspected traitor. She was given permission to take exercise within the grounds of Woodstock Manor, to receive pre-approved visitors, write and receive correspondence from outside and had access to her some of her former household. However all of these activities were monitored for signs of conspiracy.

Elizabeth spent eleven months with Beddingfield in Oxfordshire before she was called to attend her sister's court at Hampton Court during April 1555. Once again, it was Philip who Elizabeth had to thank for this recognition of her status as a member of the royal family. Mary may have allowed Elizabeth to come to court, but she refused to meet her in person. Eventually, Mary was persuaded that Elizabeth was to be trusted enough to return to her former home at Hatfield House in north London. It was here that she stayed during the remainder of Mary's reign and it was at Hatfield that she would hear the news that Mary had died, and she was the new Queen of England.

This was without doubt one of the hardest periods of Elizabeth's life, but during this time, she learnt she could be a strong, resilient woman during times of crisis. She showed great courage and strength during her interrogations by Stephen Gardiner, despite her young age and used her intelligence to keep herself safe. Elizabeth would also remember who had helped and been loyal to her during this period and she would reward them when she came to the throne. Could Elizabeth see during that final visit to court how Philip manipulated Mary even though she was the queen? Could this have helped solidify further her feelings against the idea of marriage? Having survived these troubled times and seen men and women go to their deaths, Elizabeth must have felt that she had survived all that for one reason - that she was destined to ascend the throne of England and become queen herself.

1558: The Death of Bloody Mary

It is rather ironic that Henry VIII who really wanted sons actually fathered two strong, determined women who would go on and continue the Tudor dynasty for a further fifty-six years after his death, as queens in their own right. But Mary and Elizabeth shared a toxic rivalry right up to Mary's death in 1558.

During her short reign and marriage to Philip II of Spain, Mary experienced pseudocyesis, more commonly known as phantom pregnancy, twice, once at the beginning of her reign and the second not long before her death. At 38, Mary was comparatively old by sixteenth century standards when she married Philip. Today 38 is still considered old to be having a first child, but in the sixteenth century it must have been considered very old, especially considering girls as young as 15 were conceiving children and giving birth during this time.

Evidence of Mary's rumoured condition can be found in the Calendar of State Papers, Spain, (Volume 13, 1554-1558, ed. Royall Tyler London, 1954), in an entry from 6 November 1554, from the Spanish ambassador to the Holy Roman Emperor that states: 'There is no doubt that the Queen is with child, for her stomach clearly shows it and her dresses no longer fit her.'

By April 1555, the queen entered her customary conferment ahead of her expected delivery date in May. May, June and July all passed with no sign of the queen going into labour or a baby appearing. This must have been heartbreaking for Mary as well as publicly humiliating. Eventually Mary left her confinement chamber in August 1555 pale, thin and minus a child. No one ever mentioned it to her again.

The second phantom pregnancy came after Philip (who still lived in Spain) had visited Mary for three months during the summer of 1557. When he left in mid-July, to return to Spain, Mary was sure that during their time together that she had at last conceived a much longed for

Catholic heir. Sadly, she was once again mistaken, and this was the start of a series of spells of ill health that by the end of the year would have sent her to her grave. As her time to go into confinement approached, in March 1558, even Mary realised that she was in fact probably unlikely to be with child. This in turn prompted her to make her last will and testament in the event that something went wrong either due to childbirth or from a fatal illness.

The content of her will and the subsequent will she made just before her death, no longer exists, but a transcript of them with the original Tudor spelling can be found in J. M. Stone's, Mary I: Queen of England, published in 1901 and was subsequently transcribed from the lost Harleian MSS 6949.

> 'In the name of God, Amen. I Marye by the Grace of God Quene of Englond, Spayne, France, both Sicelles, Jerusalem and Ireland, Defender of the Faythe, Archduchesse of Austriche, Duchesse of Burgundy, Millayne and Brabant, Countesse of Hapsburg, Flanders and Tyroll, and lawful wife to the most noble and virtuous Prince Philippe, by the same Grace of God Kynge of the said Realms and Domynions of Engand, &c. Thinking myself to be with child in lawful marriage between my said dearly beloved husband and Lord, altho' I be at this present (thankes be unto Almighty God) otherwise in good helthe, yet foreseeing the great danger which by Godd's ordynance remaine to all whomen in ther travel of children, have thought good, both for discharge of my conscience and continewance of good order within my Realmes and domynions to declare my last will and testament.'

Mary goes on to state that in the event of her death, that Philip II would rule as regent for their child.

> 'Neverthelesse the order, Government and Rewle of my said issewe, and of my said Imperiall Crowne, and the dependances thereof, during the Minoryte of my said heyre and Issewe, I specyally recommend unto my said most Dere and well beloved husband, accordynge to the laws of this my said Realme for the same provided. Willing, charging, and most

hertily requyryng all and singular my lovyng, obedient and naturall subjects, by that profession and-dewtye of allegiance that by God's commandment they owe unto me, beyng ther naturall Sovereigne Lady & Quene.' *(J. M. Stone's, Mary I: Queen of England, published in 1901 and was subsequently transcribed from the lost Harleian MSS 6949)*

Once again, there was no child, and the experience took its toll on Mary's delicate health. In the months running up to her final illness, Mary contracted influenza. During the 1550s, there were several waves of deadly flu epidemics that swept throughout England, causing thousands to die. Flu in the sixteenth century was much more serious than it is today as medical understanding was crude and treatments such as bleeding and the application of leeches often turned out to be far more of hindrance than a help. Despite her weakened state, Mary survived her flu, but it became clear that she was not in good health.

Mary realised that she was mortally ill by the end of October1558. This is when she did something that showed great personal strength and must have cost her emotionally and personally; she amended her will. In the amendments, she acknowledged that she was at a point in her life when she is unlikely to have an heir and she indirectly proclaimed Elizabeth as her successor without naming her, by referencing their father's, will.

'Yf yt shall please Almighty God to call me to his mercye owte of this transytory lyfe without issewe and heire of my bodye lawfully begotten, Then I most instantly desire et per viscera misericordiae Dei, requyre my next heire & Successour, by the Laws and Statutes of this Realme, not only to permytt and suffer the executors of my said Testament and last will and the Survivours of them to performe the same, and to appoynte unto them such porcyon of treasure & other thynges as shall be suffycient for the execution of my said testament and last will, and to ayd them in the performance of the same, but also yf such assurance and conveyance as the Law requyreth for the State of the londs which I have devysed and appoynted to the howses of Religion.' *(J. M. Stone's Mary I: Queen of England, published in 1901 and was transcribed from the lost Harleian MSS 6949)*

She also legally stated that her husband, Philip II of Spain had no legal duty or right to her kingdoms upon her death, but she hoped that he would support the new successor.

> 'And albeit my said most Dere Lord and Husband shall for defawte of heyre of my bodye have no further government, order and rewle within this Realme and the domynions thereunto belongynge, but the same doth and must remayne, descend, and goo unto my next heyre and Successour, accordyng to the Lawes and Statuts of this Realme, yet I most humbly beseech his Majesty, in recompence of the great love and humble dewtye that I have allwayes born and am bounden to bere unto his Majesty.' *(J. M. Stone's Mary I: Queen of England, published in 1901 and was transcribed from the lost Harleian MSS 6949)*

From spring 1558, Elizabeth had started to discreetly prepare for the future with the help of her trusty ally and friend William Cecil, whose wise council and political astuteness would last throughout Elizabeth's reign until his death in 1598. The half-sisters' relationship had been tense, with mutual suspicion on both sides. In order to survive her sister's 'bloody' counter-reformation Elizabeth had outwardly claimed to be a Catholic and had kept her head down, avoiding drawing attention to herself in anyway.

Before Mary amended her will in October 1558, Elizabeth may have had a very strong claim to the crown, but she was by no means the only candidate to be the next English monarch. The biggest of these threats came from her Catholic cousin and rival Mary Queen of Scots through their shared lineage descending from Henry VII, who was their grandfather. In fact, it was this line that would eventually inherit the throne in 1603 after Elizabeth's own death through Mary's son James I. He went on to unite Scotland and England under one monarch for the first time in the island of Britain's history.

The other less likely candidates were the surviving siblings of the ill-fated Lady Jane Grey. Mary could have nominated them as her heirs if she had chosen to honour the last wishes her brother Edward over those of their father's.

The last option that Mary could have chosen was also female; Margret Clifford, Countess of Cumberland, who was the daughter of

Eleanor Brandon, who was also the niece to Henry VIII via his sister Mary. The Countess of Cumberland would go on to become one of Elizabeth's ladies-in-waiting and had never really been a big threat to Elizabeth's ambitions for the throne. So, although Elizabeth may have been the popular, if not obvious choice, to succeed her sister, she was by no means without potential threat from other claimants.

One of the first things that Elizabeth started to do either deliberately or not was to increase the size of her household. It seems that all the noble families of England had already started to see Elizabeth as Mary's unofficial successor during the last ten months of Mary's short reign. Elizabeth, as the last surviving Protestant Tudor issue from Henry VIII, had always attracted support both publicly and clandestinely from fellow reformists across the country. Having an awareness of this support and the fact that these influential families could raise arms and men if she required it, *after* Mary's death must have been a big comfort for Elizabeth and her intimate circle.

Elizabeth was both savvy and experienced enough by this time to know that it was not wise to plan her future from her home at Hatfield Manor. Although Mary was dying, she was still technically walking that fine tight rope of treasonous activity against her sister, who had already incarcerated Elizabeth on suspicion of treason during her reign. The place used for planning Elizabeth's future was Brocket Hall, approximately three miles from Hatfield Manor. There were other good reasons for Elizabeth and her council of allies to choose Brocket Hall, its location had easy access to the River Lea, which was both a communication and escape route. It was also easier to defend than Hatfield which was made up of great sprawling gardens. The key noblemen who helped plan with Elizabeth during the dying months of Mary's reign were Sir William Cecil, Thomas Parry, Lord and Lady Clinton, the Earl of Bedford, Robert Dudley, Sir Nicolas Throckmorton, Sir Peter Carew and John Harrington.

On 28th October, Elizabeth was made aware of the amendment Mary had made to her will finally hinting at her as her successor. This good news came to Elizabeth via Jane Dormer one of Mary's intimate household. Mary however did not offer this without expecting something back from Elizabeth. The important condition set out by Mary was that Elizabeth was required to keep England Catholic, the other condition was that Elizabeth would settle any outstanding debts left by Mary upon her death. Even in 1558, Elizabeth was politically wise enough to know not to quibble with her sister over the point of religion when Mary was handing her what she wanted on a plate. Elizabeth therefore replied that she would be a good Catholic, being as ambiguous as Mary had been.

The saddest and most treacherous of Elizabeth's new allies and supporters came in the form of her brother-in-law Philip II. Philip sent an ambassador to England to bring greetings to his dying wife, to inform her government that he was happy to assist and support Elizabeth in her succession; not out of kindness but to try and control and manipulate his sister-in-law. The ambassador who Philip entrusted with this important task was the Count of Feria. After visiting the dying queen's court and doing his official business, he visited Elizabeth on the 10 November. To start with the visit went well, Feria offered Elizabeth Philip's, rather premature, congratulations and offered her assistance in the coming months, but then the ambassador made a diplomatic faux pas - he went on to say that Elizabeth owed the fact she had been named as successor solely to the intervention of Philip and that he strongly expressed a wish that she should marry Emmanuel Philibert, the Duke of Savoy. The proposed match would suit the Spanish very well and would give Philip a degree of control over his young sister-in-law once she became queen. This badly worded and blatantly obvious attempt to try and manipulate Elizabeth went on to affect the relationship between England and Spain until Philip's death in 1598. These tensions would ultimately climax at the attempted invasion of the Spanish Armada in 1588.

In the last week of Mary's life, she was in tremendous pain and drifted in and out of consiousness. The queen officially received the Catholic sacrament of the last rites from her confessor, on the evening of 16 November, 1558. Mass was celebrated within her bedchamber during the early hours of the morning on the 17 November. Queen Mary slipped away from this world later that day. She was 42-years-old. Mary and her reputed bloody reign of the English counter-reformation was finally over.

Elizabeth honoured her sister's faith to the church in Rome and arranged for her funeral to be celebrated in the Catholic tradition. The liturgy used were the same words of service used for their late father Henry VIII. It took Mary's ladies three days to prepare their mistress for her laying in state, that began on 21 November. She was presented in a lead-lined coffin covered in her personal cloth of state, within the Privy Chamber at St James Palace. All the important people of the realm were admitted to pay their last respects to the late Queen of England. Mary's body remained at St James Palace for six weeks, until on 13 December 1558 she started her last journey to her final resting place, at Westminster Abbey. The place of burial did go against Mary's final wishes; for she had hoped to lie for all eternity with her mother, Katherine of Argon, within Peterborough Cathedral. The funeral procession took the queen's coffin, covered with gold cloth and a life size effigy of Mary along Pall Mall and Charing Cross through Kings Street which brought the procession towards Whitehall and on to Westminster Abbey.

That night, a candlelit vigil took place around Mary's coffin where it stood at the high alter of the abbey. The next morning, after the requiem mass had been said, the coffin was taken to be buried within the Tudor vault of the abbey. She was placed with Henry VII. At 25, Elizabeth was now the Queen of England and about to start one of the longest reigns of British history.

PART 2

ELIZABETH THE QUEEN

'I do not so much rejoice that God hath made me to be a Queen, as to be a Queen over so thankful a people'

(Elizabeth's Golden Speech to Parliament 30 November 1601 ref: SP12/282ff.137r_141v)

1559: The Coronation of Elizabeth I & The Religious Settlement

In February 1558, when Elizabeth saw her step-sister for the last time, she may have realised that Mary was seriously unwell. By the summer of that year, it had become painfully obvious that the queen was extremely ill. But it was not until a couple of weeks before her death that Mary officially named her younger step-sister, and daughter of her late mother's enemy, Anne Boleyn, as her heir and successor to the throne. The dying queen's privy counsellors approached Mary on 6 November and asked for the queen to confirm Elizabeth as her heir. Mary had no energy left to argue against Elizabeth; she knew her time was coming to an end and so reluctantly, she agreed to their request. This reluctance was obvious when she referred to Elizabeth without using her name in the text of her will. Two days later, the Controller and the Master of the Rolls were dispatched to Hatfield House to inform Elizabeth that she was now the official heir to the throne.

Mary's suffering came to an end on the morning of Thursday, 17 November 1558 at 6:00 am at the royal residency of St James Palace in London. She had ruled for just over five years. Mary certainly had been unwell for some time, and it is highly likely that she was suffering from a cancer that affected her reproductive system. Be sure, but either way, she would have died sooner rather than later.

It was the duty of the Earls of Pembroke and Arundel to go to Hatfield House and inform Elizabeth that she was now officially the Queen of England. When they arrived, Elizabeth was out in the gardens of Hatfield. Upon hearing that Mary was dead, she fell to her knees and is reported to have exclaimed: 'A Domino factum et illud et est mirabile in Oculis nostril' which translates as: This is the Lord's doing and it is marvellous to our ears'.

76

Parliament was informed of the death of Mary and the accession of Elizabeth on 17 November by the Lord Chancellor, Nicholas Heath. Heath said the following to the congregated members of the late queen's government:

> 'Which hap as it is most heavy and grievous unto us, so have we no less cause another way to rejoice with praise to Almighty God for that He hath left unto us a true, lawful and right inheritrices to the crown of this realm, Which Lady Elizabeth, of whose lawful right and title we need not doubt. Wherefore the lords of this house have determined with your assents and consents, to pass from hence into the palace, and there to proclaim the said Lady Elizabeth Queen of this realm without further tract of time.' *(Holinshed Rafael Chronicles vol 4, pub 1807-8)*

The transition of power from Henry VIII's eldest daughter to his youngest can be described as smooth. There are several reasons for this seamless succession; the first being that one of Elizabeth's biggest foes, Cardinal Reginald Pole died a few hours after Mary. This in turn made Elizabeth's religious reforms easier to implement as there was little opposition. Elizabeth also had the advantage of being the daughter of Henry VIII and was English rather than Scottish. The nearest contender for the crown after Elizabeth had been her cousin Mary Stuart, Queen of Scots. At the time of Elizabeth's succession, the Queen of Scots was the daughter-in-law of England's foe, the King of France. Although Mary Stuart was Catholic like the late queen - even the English Catholics found it hard, at this time, to support a Scot, living in France so soon after the loss, earlier that year, of the former English territory in France - Calais. The English had also recently been defeated in the Franco-Spanish War, led by the late queen's husband Philip II. So, the majority of English Catholics simply hoped that Elizabeth would be tolerant and would not start a reign of persecution as her two half-siblings had done.

Elizabeth remained at Hatfield House until 23 November when she relocated to Charterhouse, just outside of the boundaries of the City of London. She was warmly greeted by the public on this first unofficial journey as the Queen of England. She remained at Charterhouse, gathering her new court and ministers around her for five days, before officially progressing to the Tower of London. This must have felt like a truly triumphant and exhilarating moment for Elizabeth who had lost her mother in this fortress and had herself been held there as a political prisoner, also fearing for her life, only a few years before. The moment of Elizabeth's jubilant arrival at The Tower was recorded by the contemporary poet, playwright and writer, John Haywood. He claims that Elizabeth said the following words to her closest attendants:

> 'Some have fallen from being princes of this land to be prisoners in this place; I am raised from being a prisoner in this place to be prince of this land. that dejection was a work of God's justice; this advancement is a work of His mercy.'
> *(Hayward, John; Annals of the first four years of the reign of Elizabeth, Ed Bruce, John, Camden Society 1840)*

Elizabeth's Coronation ring, the ring that represented that she had married her to her subjects, held a secret locket with an enamel depiction of her mother, Anne Boleyn. This moment in Elizabeth's life meant that Anne had finally triumphed over both her predecessor Katherine of Aragon and her successor Jane Seymour; for her daughter had succeeded both of their children and went on to become Henry VIII's most successful heir.

Within a fortnight, Elizabeth had relocated her expanding court to the Palace of Whitehall for her first Christmas as Queen of England. But before she was formally crowned, the new queen felt that she needed to try to settle one of the biggest issues of the sixteenth century by establishing the formal religion of her new realm. The outline of the Act of Supremacy was created in the last weeks of 1558 and was officially formalised in 1559. This new act brought back the supreme authority of the church within England to the reigning monarch, making Elizabeth the supreme head of the Church of England. This meant that the queen and not the pope had the final say over the Christian religion practised within Elizabeth's realm. This act needed to redefine what was heresy under this new denomination of faith. It also had to reintroduce the use of an Oath of Supremacy, to be sworn by all men taking an official office within Elizabeth's household, government and council.

The next time these laws would be revised was during the 1670s under the guise of the Test Acts during the restoration court of Charles II; and then again, during the joint reign of William and Mary, after the disastrously short Catholic reign of James II. Each deployment of this oath, both in the sixteenth and seventeenth century, was to achieve the same aim and to show a united Anglican presence at the heart of the ruling class and court. The enduring hope was that the populous would not fear an infiltration of Catholicism via those in charge and close to the monarch.

Although Elizabeth reintroduced the Protestant faith, she did so in a uniquely English way - the liturgy and prayers were Protestant, but the services were traditionally more Catholic in feel compared to those that had been favoured by her step-brother Edward VI. Services and churches once again had candles and incense and vicars wore vestments simular to the Catholic clergy. There was even the use of religious music, something that the new queen was particularly fond of listening to. Elizabeth hoped her Church of England would be a comfortable compromise to both her Protestant and Catholic subjects; by balancing the new and traditional elements of the Christian faith to encourage tolerance. Indeed, Elizabeth famously said, 'I have no desire to make windows into men's souls.' And for the first part of her rule there was a tolerance that had not been seen in either the reigns of her two half-siblings. It would be a mixture of events and the influence of her two prominent ministers, Sir Francis Walsingham and William Cecil (later Lord Burghley) that would lead to a more anti-Catholic, more reformist policy, using both Elizabeth's personal safety and the stability of the country as justification.

As 1558 drew to a close, and with the queen's first Christmas at Whitehall behind her, Elizabeth needed to focus on her imminent coronation. As per the tradition of the day, she moved from Whitehall back to the Tower of London, forty-eight hours before the ceremony at Westminster Abbey. Today, the new monarch processes from Buckingham Palace, rather than The Tower, to the Abbey. Elizabeth travelled to The Tower via the River Thames, accompanied by many of her new court and important officials from the City of London. At 2:00 pm on 15 January 1559, Elizabeth started to move through the crowds within a litter coach decorated with cloth of gold. It was a snowy, cold and wet January day, but thousands of Londoners had come out to see their new queen and to enjoy the pageants and free wine along the route to the Abbey. The route she took went via Fenchurch Street, Cornhill, along Cheapside towards old St Paul's, then up Fleet Street, close to the Inns of Court and Temple Bar. By the time Elizabeth reached Westminster Abbey, the short January day was fading, and the litter required torch light to guide it for the last part of the journey. At the entrance of the Abbey, the queen had a walkway made of purple cloth to bring her into the building and the sacred ceremony that would marry her to her realm until her death.

There had been controversy over who was to officiate over Elizabeth's coronation as all the English Church's hierarchy at the time of Mary's death had naturally been Catholic. As Bishop Pole, the Archbishop of Canterbury had died only hours after the late queen, the next highest bishop in the land was the Archbishop of York, Nicholas Heath, who in turn refused to lead the service on the grounds of Elizabeth's reformist views. Eventually the Elizabethan court was able to find a bishop willing to undertake the honour of leading the coronation service and he was the Bishop of Carlisle, Owen Oglethorpe.

During the first part of the service, Elizabeth was proclaimed the queen from all four directions of the Abbey. She was then led to the high altar upon the Cosmati Pavement that still is the traditional place, within the abbey, used for the coronation of monarchs in England today. Here, the new queen kneeled before the Bishop of Carlisle and offered him gold. The next part of the ceremony was conducted in English and is known as the Bidding of the People's Prayer. Simple language was used so that the people of the realm could hear and understand the promises and oaths sworn by Elizabeth, both in her role as the queen and also as the head of the Anglican Church.

The climax of the service followed when Elizabeth, who was now seated on St Edward's chair, the thirteenth century throne placed on the Cosmati Pavement, was anointed and crowned monarch. At a time when kings and queens felt they were God's appointed representatives this was considered the most scared and important part of the whole ceremony. Until this point in the service, Elizabeth had worn a red high-collared gown with a matching cap and an ermine cape - now she needed to change into a lighter gown made of rich cloth of gold, out of sight, within a small side chapel of the minister. The bishop then proceeded to anoint her with holy oil on the palms of her hands and upon her chest, between her shoulder blades, on the inside of her elbows and lastly, her forehead. Next, she pulled on a pair of white gloves and received the sceptre and orb, before three crowns were placed on her head. The first was the crown of Edward the Confessor, which was followed by the State Crown and then the small crown that had been made especially for her brother, Edward VI.

Trumpets were sounded as a signal to the public that the new queen had officially been crowned, and then mass was celebrated. Before leaving the abbey as the new Queen of England, Elizabeth changed for a third time, this time into robes of royal purple and ermine furs taking the first official steps of her forty-five stoic years upon the throne of England.

Shortly after her coronation, the anxieties of her counsellors, especially those of William Cecil and Francis Walsingham, would be forced to refocus on Elizabeth's potentially dangerous rivals for her throne, when she made it clear that she would not marry in a speech made on 10 February 1559.

> 'And albeit it might please almighty God to continue me still in this mind to live out of the state of marriage, yet it is not to be feared … whereby the realm shall not remain destitute of an heir... And in the end this shall be for me sufficient, that a marble stone shall declare that a Queen, having reigned such a time, lived and died a virgin.'

Having helped to ensure that Elizabeth had successfully been crowned Cecil, Walshingham and their colleagues on the privy council had to help her keep the throne and thrive as a monarch. Elizabeth had learnt much from both of her siblings' short and troubled reigns and she had chosen to learn from their errors when forming her views on succession, for she knew that had Edward lived or Mary had children, she wouldn't have been on the throne in the first place, and it was a position that she intended to keep. This goal, above anything else, shaped her feelings towards marriage and her views on faith. Blessed with her Tudor looks, her mother's temperament and her humanist education, Elizabeth was naturally equipped to be one of the strongest and most successful monarchs of British history.

1560: The Mysterious Death of Amy Robsart

Elizabeth I was an expert in understanding the power of her image and the importance of the reputation of both herself and her courtiers. She had seen first-hand how rumour and bad reputation had been the downfall of not just her mother, but also some of her mother's successors. Therefore, any hint or suspicion of scandal amongst her courtiers needed to be dealt with swiftly and she needed to be seen to distance herself from any controversy in the most public of ways; even when this meant banishing one of her favourite courtiers.

Historians have debated, analysed and speculated for centuries on the relationship between Elizabeth and her court favourite, Robert Dudley throughout her reign – but the only definitive answer is that we will never know if their relationship was purely platonic or if they were more intimate than just good friends.

Dudley came from a landed, gentrified family and he was the fifth son of the first Duke of Northumberland. Robert Dudley. He had been a childhood friend of both Elizabeth and her younger brother, Edward VI. All three had been schooled under the same tutor, Roger Ascham. As the fifth son of a duke, Robert would not have inherited much from his father, so one way of improving his prospects and wealth would have been to marry into a wealthy family.

Amy Dudley nee Robsart was the only heiress to a wealthy landlord in Norfolk by the name of Sir John Robsart, and his wife Elizabeth. She was born on 7 June 1532 in Oxford. Like her contemporaries Lady Jane Grey and Lady Elizabeth, Amy had received a humanist education and was of the new reformist Protestant faith. Not much else is known about her early life.

It is believed that Robert and Amy married for love or maybe lust, rather than through a pre-arrangement made by their parents. The match may have been the personal choice of the couple but fortunately, both families approved. Their short courtship lasted just under a year and they married on 4 June 1550; three days shy of the bride's eighteenth birthday. The marriage ceremony and feast took place at the now lost Tudor Palace of Sheen and they even had Edward VI and his sister Lady Elizabeth as their guests.

During the reign of Elizabeth's step-sister 'Bloody' Mary, both Elizabeth and Dudley found themselves incarcerated in the Tower of London at the same time. Robert Dudley was also Lady Jane Grey's brother-in-law through marriage. This connection to the nine-day queen put Dudley under grave suspicion from Queen Mary.

Elizabeth and Dudley had many shared interests and life experiences in common. Not only had they been educated together, but they'd both lost a parent at the scaffold, and on a lighter note, they shared reformist religious beliefs and both loved hunting and dancing.

Also during Mary's reign, Elizabeth's finances were extremely tight, and she soon found herself in debt. It was Dudley and not her sister, the queen, who helped her out. He sold some of his lands and gave Elizabeth the funds from these sales to ease her financial difficulties. Due to this generous and chivalrous act, the Dudleys were forced to live modestly upon Robert's release from The Tower until Amy received her inheritance in 1557. The couple lodged with family and friends with a very modest household of people for a couple of their class and status. Their finances were improved again in the summer of 1557, when Dudley undertook military service for the consort king of England, Philip II of Spain. He took part in the Spanish victory of St Quentin off the coast of France, which took place on 10 August 1557. This battle was a particularly bloody defeat for the French and Dudley was rewarded for his part in the battle.

Upon her accession to the throne, Elizabeth was determined to reward her 'Robin' for his friendship and support during some of the hardest periods of her life. First, she ennobled him, giving Dudley the title of the Earl of Leicester and made him her Master of the Horse, a prestigious and highly sought-after position within court. Dudley's new role granted him frequent access to the queen, however Elizabeth caused further controversy and sparked scandalous rumours when she had his court chambers moved next to her own, so that the friends could meet at any time of the day or night. For an unmarried 'Virgin Queen' to behave thus towards a married courtier, was not just seen as brazen and scandalous within her own court but within Catholic Europe too. Reports of her conduct by gossip loving ambassadors spread rumours about Elizabeth's affection and blatant favouritism towards her Master of the Horse. However, the closeness of their controversial relationship ended in abruptly in 1560 when Leicester's first wife, Amy died suddenly in rather mysterious circumstances at the age of 29.

Over a year before her death, the Spanish ambassador made comment in the Calendar of State Papers for Spain about Amy Dudley's health stating she had 'a malady in one of her breasts' *(CSP Spanish 1558-67 P56-58)*. In 1559, a similar comment was made in correspondence that can be found in the Venetian Calendar of State papers by the ambassador who notes cynically and cruelly 'His [Dudley] wife, who has been ailing for some time, were perchance to die, the Queen might easily take him for a husband.' *(CSP Venetian 1558-80 P69)*. It is worth noting here that it was not customary for the spouses of courtiers to attend court if they did not hold a position at court themselves this goes to explain why Amy did not often attend court with her husband.

On 8 September 1560 Lady Amy Dudley was residing at a property owned by Anthony Forster, esq. who was leasing his property to the Dudley's acquaintance, William Owen. The property was known as Cumnor Place and was located within Oxfordshire. Very little is known about the day in question, however, what is known is that Amy gave the small household staff permission to go to a local fair being held at nearby Abingdon. When the staff returned to the house, they found their mistress at the bottom of the main staircase, dead from a broken neck. Although in ill health, Amy's death was unexpected and very sudden. Due to her husband's closeness to the queen, it would provoke questions and scandalous gossip rather sympathy for the late Lady Dudley, The Earl of Leicester and the queen herself.

The incriminating circumstance surrounding Amy's sudden death was that she had sent the staff away that day. Had she intended to take her life? If so, was that because she was increasingly ill and lonely and saw it as a way out? Did she do it to free the man she had married for love so he could pursue the queen? Or did she know what the consequence of her actions would be and had she hoped to punish her husband for abandoning her for Elizabeth? Maybe she had simply sought peace and quiet from the servants and some unscrupulous assassin, hired by any

An example of Elizabeth I's signature, found on all official documents. (Public domain)

Iryſhe.	Latten.	Engliſhe,
Coneŗ ca cu.	Quomodo habes,	How doe you.
Caim ʒo maih.	Bene ſum.	I am well,
ʒo ŗo maih aʒaɒ.	Habeo gratias,	I thancke you,
In eol ɒŗc ʒealaʒ	Poſſis ne ~ ~ ~ ꜰ	Cann you ~ ~ ꜰ
ɒo Lanuŗɒ. ~ ~ ꜰ	hibernice loqui ꜰ	speake Jryſhe
Ꝺ baŗ lavɒen.	Dic latine.	Speake Latten
Ꝺɩꝺ Le ŗiuean ꜰ	Deus adiuat ~ ~ ꜰ	God saue the
ŗároɲa ~ ~ ~ ꜰ	Reginā Angliæ ꜰ	Queene off
		Englande:

Above: An Irish Latin English translation made by Elizabeth between 1560-80. (Public domain)

Below: The funeral of Elizabeth I (1603). The casket of the late Elizabeth I is accompanied by mourners bearing the Tudor heraldic banners. Artist unknown. (Public domain)

Lady Elizabeth, circa 1546,
oil on oak, accredited
to William Scrots.
(Public domain)

The artist of this portrait
of Elizabeth I is unknown.
It is estimated to date from
around 1575. Oil on panel.
(Public domain)

A portrait of Elizabeth's mother, Anne Boleyn, by the most esteemed court painter of his time, Hans Holbein. (Public domain)

The most iconic image of Elizabeth's father, Henry VIII, painted by Hans Holbein. Oil on canvas, dated after 1537. (Public domain)

This is a portrait of Elizabeth's sister Mary I, attributed to Hans Eworth. Oil on canvas, dated between 1555-58. (Public domain)

Elizabeth's brother Edward VI, with his maternal uncles, Thomas and Edward Seymour. Artist unknown, dated 1547. (Public domain)

This is a depiction of Mary Queen of Scots, Elizabeth's cousin and rival queen. The painting is estimated to have been created between 1560-1587. Artist unknown. (Public domain)

This image of Robert Dudley, Earl of Leicester dates from 1564 and is a composition of oil on panel. The portrait shows the earl's coat of arms as well as his regalia, showing that he is part of the Order of the Garter as well as the Order of St Michael. Details may have been added after 1564, to depict honours latterly bestowed. (Public domain)

Above: It is thought that Marcus Gheeraets may be the artist responsible for this picture. It depicts Elizabeth and Leicester dancing La Volta, a somewhat risqué court dance of the 16th century. It is thought to date from about 1580. (Public domain)

CATHARINA REGINA VXOR HENRICI VIII

Left: This is Katherine Parr, painted by Hans Eworth, thought to date from 1548. Katherine was Henry VIII's sixth and final wife. Katherine's modest black dress reflects her Protestant faith. (Public domain)

D. PHILIPPVS II. CATHOLICVS, D.G. HIS=
PANIARVM, INDIARVM, ETC. REX, DVX
BRABANT. COMES FLANDRIÆ, ETC.
Anton. Wierx fecit et excud.

Printed woodcut image of
Philip II of Spain, Elizabeth's
brother in law and later opponent
during the Spanish Armada
in 1688. Artist unknown.
(Public domain)

Sir Francis Walsingham
was Elizabeth's spymaster
and one of her chief
ministers. This painting by
John de Critz features oil
on panel and can be dated
to 1585. (Public domain)

Elizabeth's most loyal and trusted confidante and minister, William Cecil, Lord Burghley. Painted by Marcus Gheeraets, this piece showcases Cecil's Order of the Garter robes and is dated between 1585 and 1598. The coat of arms in the top right hand corner may have been added after the painting was completed. (Public domain)

The artist of this rare depiction of the nine day queen, Lady Jane Grey, is unknown. It is thought to have been painted fifty years after her execution in 1554. The small prayerbook in her hand hints at her education and strong Protestant faith. (Public domain)

number of Elizabethan plotters including Dudley himself, the queen or even William Cecil, had then taken advantage of the staff being out and pushed Amy down the staircase? Or did she have a simple accident and lose her footing and simply fall to her death? Unfortunately, the truth died with Amy and it will never be known.

On the 9 September 1560, Dudley wrote to his cousin Thomas Blount telling him that one of his wife's servants had rushed to him at court, then located at Windsor Castle, with the news of his wife's sudden and suspicious death:

> 'Cousin Blount, immediately upon your departing from me there came to me Bowes by whom I understand that my wife is dead, and, as he saith, by a fall from a pair of stairs. Little other understanding can I have of him. The greatness and the sadness of the misfortune doth so perplex me, until I do hear from you how the matter standeth, or how this evil should light upon me considering what the malicious world will bruit, as I can take no rest.' *(Skidmore C, Death & the Virgin P 203)*

As is usual in the event of a sudden and unexplained death, a coroner named John Pudsey of the county of Oxfordshire and a jury of peers were called to Cumnor Place to examine the circumstances of the late Lady Amy's death. The original report held at the National Archives is written in Latin as all legal documents of the time were, but below is a copy transcribed into English:

> 'Jurors say under oath that the aforesaid Lady Amy on 8 September in the aforesaid second year of the reign of the said lady queen, being alone in a certain chamber within the home of a certain Anthony Forster, esq., in the aforesaid Cumnor, and intending to descend the aforesaid chamber by way of certain steps (in English called 'steyres') of the aforesaid chamber there and then accidentally fell precipitously down the aforesaid steps to the very bottom of the same steps, through which the same Lady Amy there and then sustained not only two injuries to her head (in English called 'dyntes') – one of which was a quarter of

an inch deep and the other two inches deep – but truly also, by reason of the accidental injury or of that fall and of Lady Amy's own body weight falling down the aforesaid stairs, the same Lady Amy there and then broke her own neck, on account of which certain fracture of the neck the same Lady Amy there and then died instantly; and the aforesaid Lady Amy was found there and then without any other mark or wound on her body; and thus the jurors say on their oath that the aforesaid Lady Amy in the manner and form aforesaid by misfortune came to her death and not otherwise, as they are able to agree at present.' *(KB9/1073/f.80 National Archives Kew)*

From reading the transcription of the report, the coroner and the jury of peers found that Amy had died by misadventure and was neither killed nor did they feel that she had committed suicide. For both Dudley and the queen this was the best possible outcome - although it may not have been the most honest.

Finally, on Sunday, 22 September 1560, Amy Dudley was laid to rest in the Oxford church of Our Lady. Prior to burial, her body had been lying in state as a member of the nobility, in what is now the college of Worcester. At the front of her funeral procession, was Amy's stepbrother, John Appleyard, who set the pace of the sombre journey whilst carrying the family's coat of arms. Her coffin was carried by eight yeomen and followed up by an escort of eighty poor men and women to the church. The procession of poor mourners was followed by members from the university's staff. Next came the church choir and finally the clergy who were to officiate at the mournful ceremony. It must have been quite a grand sight for the people of sixteenth century Oxford to witness. It is thought that the final ceremony of Lady Amy Dudley's life cost Robert Dudley an estimated two thousand pounds which was a staggering sum of money at the time. Unfortunately, the scandal and controversy surrounding Robert Dudley's wife did not end with her burial.

Upon first reading the extract from Dudley's letter to his cousin Blount it looks as if he is upset about the death of his wife. However, if you read deeper into the last part of the extract it becomes clear that he is more worried about his reputation and the gossip surrounding his late wife's passing, almost seeing it as an inconvenience rather than a huge source of grief. It seems he had reason to worry. New rumours emerged that Elizabeth had ordered the 'accident' so that she could marry her 'Robin' or that Leicester himself had arranged for his wife to be murdered so that he could marry the queen; thus, potentially making him the most powerful man of the realm. Either way, these rumours were dangerous to both the queen and her favourite. In order to quash them and to survive, Elizabeth knew that she had to distance herself from her dearest friend. Robert Dudley's absence from court did not last long and he was back at the queen's side by October of that year; although he continued to dress in black mourning clothes until the spring of the following year.

Although Elizabeth was still in her twenties and in the early part of her reign, she was able to draw on all the lessons she had learnt from her childhood as well as her own experiences of witnessing scandal within the reigns of both her siblings. As a consequence, she knew she needed to cut her 'Robin' free and distance herself from scandal. She would also use this experience and the lessons she had learnt from it to try and advise Mary Queen of Scots when her second husband was found murdered in 1567. Elizabeth counselled her cousin to distance herself from the scandal and the man associated with it. Mary foolishly ignored that advice and found herself seeking help from Elizabeth not long afterwards. This event taught Elizabeth that she had to be tough, even if it meant sacrificing something important to her, in this case, her friendship with Dudley. Also, if there had been any chance that Elizabeth hoped to marry Dudley in the future, this episode definitely ruled that out.

1561: The Return of Mary Queen of Scots from France

Mary Stuart, Queen of Scots, had found herself Queen of Scotland at just six-days-old, when her father, James V of Scotland, had died. Her mother, French-born Mary of Guise, managed to secure the role of regent to rule for her royal daughter. She had signed the Treaty of Greenwich, in 1543, that agreed the little queen should marry Prince Edward and move to England when she was 10-years-old; but this treaty was not destined to be honoured. Henry's behaviour after the treaty was signed had changed has had his relations between the old rivals, England and Scotland. This rivalry was exaggerated when the English attacked Scottish merchant ships heading to France. The Scottish Parliament felt this was unacceptable behaviour and went on to reject the Greenwich Treaty. This broken treaty gave the French a new opportunity to hurt England further when Henri II, reached out to Mary's French mother, and a new treaty was drawn up between the Dauphin (the French heir to the throne) and little Queen Mary. On 7 August 1548, five-year-old Mary Stuart, Queen of Scots, sailed to France to eventually marry the French Dauphin for what Mary Guise hoped would be a safer and happier future for her daughter than the one at the Tudor court.

Little Mary grew up within the French court, under the care and guardianship of her future father-in-law, Henri II who treated the little Scottish Queen as if she was one of his own children. Mary married the Dauphin, François, on 24 April 1558, when she was 15-years-old, at the majestic, gothic Cathedral of Notre Dame within the heart of Paris. Fifteen months after her marriage to France's Dauphin, Henri II died suddenly on 10 July 1559. He was aged just 40-years-old and Mary's new husband was now King François II of France and Mary became his consort.

Although Mary had got on well with her late father-in-law, she was not on such good terms with her mother-in-law, Catherine de Medici. Upon the death of Henri II, Mary's maternal Guise uncles, the Cardinal of Lorraine and the Duke of Guise, helped their niece's new husband to seize full power from his overbearing and controlling mother. With her son now in full control, Catherine assumed that his wife Mary must have at least had knowledge of the Coup d'état. Regardless of whether Mary had been aware of the plan or not, it would be to Mary's detriment as Catherine kept this grudge against her daughter-in-law indefinitely.

In the winter of 1560, François II became fatally ill. On 16 November, the young king passed out and his health began to deteriorate; within three weeks, on the 5 December 1560, France had lost a second king, in as many years. The exact cause of François's death is unknown, but guesses have included a serious ear infection that spread to the brain as well as the possibility that the king had contracted meningitis. Mary had been the consort of France for just seventeen months and was now a widow, just shy of her eighteenth birthday. Her mother-in-law Catherine de Medici was not going to make her life easy now François was dead. Upon her son's death, Catherine de Medici sought to finally put Mary and her Guise family back in their political place, and in doing so, was able to regain her control over France and the royal court by making a political alliance with Antoine de Bourbon and by standing in as regent for her next eldest son, 10-year-old, Charles IX, the new King of France.

With little position left within the French court, Mary decided to return to her native country of Scotland. She arrived back on Scottish soil, on 19 August 1561. If she had been expecting a warm welcome from her subjects and politicians, she was to be disappointed. Much had changed politically and religiously while she had been in France. Scotland had undergone a religious reformation and unlike the English schism, the Scottish reformation had been more reformist and closer to the doctrines of Luther than the Henrician reforms south of the boarder.

During her late husband's short reign, the Treaty of Edinburgh (1560) had been drawn up between England, France and Scotland. Near the end of her regency, Mary of Guise had faced a political and religious crisis with the new Scottish Protestants. They disliked the queen's mother for her gender, French nationality and Catholic faith. While Catholic, 'Bloody' Mary Tudor had been on the English throne, the Scottish

Protestants had been more prudent in their reforms and they hoped to find a new Protestant ally in Elizabeth I when she eventually ascended to the throne, in late 1558.

In the final year of her regency, Mary of Guise faced Protestant opposition led by her late husband's illegitimate son, James Stewart, 1st Earl of Moray. He was the leader of the Protestant Scottish movement known as the Lords of Congregation. They sought to weaken the French-Catholic alliance to Scotland through Mary of Guise and the marriage of their anointed queen by replacing them with a new Protestant alliance with Elizabeth. One of the Lords of Congregations' aims was to remove the presence of French troops on Scottish soil that had been based in the city of Leith since their young queen had set sail for her new life in France in 1548. At the peak of the political and religious crisis during 1560, joint Scottish and English Protestant armed men forced these French troops into a siege, within the eastern Scottish coastal town. The stand-off came to an end and the Treaty of Edinburgh was formed. However, during the negotiation talks, on 11 June 1560, Mary of Guise died of dropsy and the Earl of Moray took over the Scottish negotiations for his step-sister Mary, Queen of Scots.

The Edinburgh Treaty managed to achieve the Protestants' goals of sending the French troops back to France and strengthening the relationship with England. Moray had negotiated a position of power for Scotland, but that influence would only last while his step-sister Mary remained in France. Mary's return after François's death meant that there would be new political and religious unrest in Scotland which concerned Elizabeth.

The return of Mary to Scotland also brought the English Catholics a new figurehead and fresh hope for influence. This was especially true as Mary was the next best heir to the English throne, after Henry VIII's children. Mary was Henry VII's great granddaughter. Henry VIII had been Mary's great-uncle and his sister, Margret Tudor, had been her grandmother. This family connection made the English and Scottish queens cousins once removed. Mary's return to the British Isles would have struck alarm bells for both Cecil and Walsingham. With Elizabeth refusing to take a husband, the two courtiers knew Mary posed a potential risk to the Protestant soul of the English nation.

Unlike her cousin Elizabeth, Mary was soon looking for another husband. This too caused Elizabeth and her two trusted courtiers, Cecil and Walsingham, to worry. What if Mary married into Catholic

European royalty? Having just made peace with France and getting them on good terms as an ally against Spain, this could pose a serious threat to the relative religious tolerance Elizabeth's England had achieved. One of Elizabeth's solutions was to suggest that Mary marry Elizabeth's favourite, the widowed Robert Dudley, Earl of Leicester. For Elizabeth to offer up her 'Robin' to her rival must have been very hard indeed. Unsurprising, Mary refused Elizabeth's suggestion of Dudley and her advice and instead eventually settled not on a European Catholic, but an English Catholic and a mutual relation to both queens, their cousin Henry Stuart, Lord Darnley. Darnley was descended from both James II of Scotland and Henry VII of England, through Margaret Tudor. He was also the heir to the Lennox earldom within Scotland. Elizabeth was not thrilled with Mary's choice of spouse and even tried to dissuade her cousin from the match, but ultimately, she could not stop the union. Although he was a prominent member of both the English and Scottish aristocracy before his marriage, Mary made him the Earl of Ross as well as bestowing him the dukedom of Albany in his own right. Mary had married for politics with her first brief marriage, but it could be argued that her second marriage was a union of her choosing.

Darnley has been described as charming, youthful, dashing and handsome and in his very brief courtship of the Queen of Scots, he behaved well. He arrived at the Scottish court in February 1565 and was marrying the queen in July of that same year. The marriage took place on 29 July, and unlike her first marriage, this was a small, private affair held in her chapel at Holyroodhouse, Edinburgh. As soon as the marriage was legal, Darnley let his true colours show, as he did not even attend his marriage mass with his new wife. Mary had just legally bound herself to one of the biggest mistakes of her life.

Arrogant, pompous and promiscuous with both men and women, Darnley would show off and abuse his new position. His behaviour did not make him popular with the Protestant and sombre men of Mary's council. Darnley was too young and vain to care what the council or his new wife thought. As a result of his libertine lifestyle, he was often ill with symptoms of syphilis and he even passed this sexually transmitted disease onto the queen. Although the marriage was not the fairytale that Mary had hoped for, she soon found herself pregnant.

One of the ways that Mary coped with her second husband's wild behaviour was to have a trusted circle of people around her, including her personal secretary, a fellow Catholic, David Rizzio. The pair would work on official state business, but Mary also enjoyed the Italian's company as a friend as well. Darnley, however, was not a fan of his wife's personal secretary or the amount of time that they spent together, and he soon grew jealous of how close they were. He was also angry at Mary for refusing to make him a Crown Matrimonial, granting him equal power to her own. This would have meant that the Scottish throne would have passed to him if she had died before giving birth to an heir.

Vanity, anger and jealousy were a dangerous combination and they were the driving forces that made Darnley plot a vicious revenge upon his wife. On the evening of 9 March 1566, Darnley and several of his friends broke uninvited into the queen's private chambers and proceeded to viciously attack and kill David Rizzio in front of a heavily pregnant Mary. The attack was unprovoked, savage and his dead body bore the evidence of fifty-six stab wounds. Mary would never forgive Darnley for what he did that tragic night.

Despite the shock and horror of the murder of her friend and secretary, Mary carried her child to full term and gave birth to a healthy baby boy on 19 June 1566. Her son James would become James VI of Scotland and later James I of England. Mary and Darnley now lived increasingly separate lives.

Mary's return to the British Isles had stirred up the underlying religious friction that had been present within England since Elizabeth's father had broken away from Rome in order to marry her mother. Mary would prove to be a weak and ineffectual monarch within her Scottish court and this in turn made her a liability to the peace south of the boarder. Mary had further threatened Elizabeth's England by marrying an English Catholic with legitimate claims to the English throne in his own right. This made future policies made by Elizabeth's privy council more anti-Catholic in nature than they had been during her earlier reign, and they would become increasingly less tolerant as Mary's fortunes declined.

1562: The Smallpox

One of the biggest crises of Elizabeth's early reign happened during October 1562 when the queen contracted one of the sixteenth century's deadliest killers - smallpox. The young queen's near fatal experience highlighted the fact that she had no Tudor successor to take the throne should she die from such a life-threatening disease. As a consequence of her illness, the issue of the need of an heir would become one of the longest lasting personal and political battles between Elizabeth and her council during her long reign.

In the weeks before Elizabeth's illness, several members of her court had contracted and sadly succumbed to the deadly airborne virus. On 10 October, Elizabeth is said to have complained of feeling unwell. Nobody at this point suspected the queen of having smallpox as she was missing the infection's recognisable red rash. In an attempt to feel better, the queen requested a bath, but over the next six days, she steadily grew sicker until on 16 October she was so ill that she was unable to speak. Both her doctors and counsellors started to prepare for the worst possible outcome; no one expected Elizabeth to recover as the court started to plan for the future.

In a last-ditch attempt to revive the queen's discomfort, a German physician of some note was called to examine her. His name was Kranich Burchard, but he was popularly known as Dr Burcot. After accessing Elizabeth, the German doctor wrapped Elizabeth in red cloth and placed her close to a raging fire. Within two hours, the queen was able to speak again and Burcot received 100 marks for treating her. Elizabeth was, it seems, very aware of how close she'd come to dying as she immediately informed her counsellors of her strange and daring choice of successor should she die. The person she named as heir was her court favourite Robert Dudley. Thankfully for the counsellors and history, over the coming days the queen's condition steadily improved and her last wish was not required to be fulfilled. By the 25 October, the queen was starting to attend to the business of state again. Elizabeth was very fortunate that the physical scars from her smallpox were minor and were easily concealed using the early forms of make-up available to wealthy sixteenth century women, such as crushed lead paste.

The fall-out of her illness politically however would haunt the rest of her reign. Elizabeth had witnessed and experienced what it was like to be the nominated or to be the assumed heir to the crown. In a post-reformation England, a potential heir could attract fanatics and plots in line with their religious convictions. When Edward VI named Lady Jane Grey as his heir this caused a major crisis and ultimately, resulted in more plots being hatched from the losing Grey side, and the brutal execution of a young woman. While waiting in the successional wings, Elizabeth herself had attracted plots directly or indirectly during Mary's Catholic reign. This episode had brought Elizabeth perilously close to the same fate as her mother, Anne Boleyn. She managed to survive through, distancing herself from any plots planned in her name and outwardly changing her religious conviction to appease her sister Mary. This experience was why Elizabeth was so was reluctant to put someone else in the same position, it was for both their safety as well as her own.

Elizabeth's frustrated privy counsellors had struggled to find an appropriate candidate to succeed her during her illness, and they now put pressure on the queen to consider taking a husband as soon as possible, in order to produce a Protestant heir to continue the Tudor line. Despite having no less than thirty men seeking her hand in marriage during her reign, including her former brother-in-law, Philip II of Spain, Archduke Charles of Austria and Eric XIV of Sweden, none were able to convince Elizabeth that they were worthy of being her husband. Elizabeth knew that she would never find a man who was equal to her position. She had seen the disastrous long-distance marriage of her sister Mary and was understandably unwilling to accept an international monarch of equal rank as a potential groom.

After accepting that Elizabeth would remain the 'Virgin Queen' Cecil and Walsingham became focused on discovering plots against the monarch, and specifically plots involving directly or indirectly Mary Queen of Scots, who was, they felt, the mostly likely unconfirmed candidate for the throne. The Queen of Scots did become for many English Catholics, a symbol of religious hope for the future when she turned to Elizabeth for help. This in turn was made worse when English Catholics were encouraged to start plotting against Elizabeth after Pope Pius V issued a papal bull against Elizabeth in 1570. Therefore, Elizabeth's smallpox had bigger implications than whether she lived or died, the episode had scared her government and influenced the political agenda of her privy council and governments to varying degrees, for the rest of her reign. Rarely are matters such as grief or illness kept as private matters for monarchs.

1567: The Death of Lord Darnley

Relations between Mary Queen of Scots and her second husband, Henry Stuart, Lord Darnley never recovered after the brutal murder of David Rizzio, Mary's personal secretary. With the birth of baby James, Mary had produced an important male heir and there was no reason to resume marital relations with Darnley for the time being.

David Rizzio's murder was not just down to jealousy, it was about punishing Mary for her refusal to create Darnley the Crown Matrimonial. Darnley claimed this humiliated him as a man and as her husband because Mary had a higher status than him. Darnley definitely had masculinity issues, but this was not uncommon in sixteenth century men. Several of the attackers who had taken part in the murder of Rizzio had already prudently fled from Scotland for the sanctuary of mainland Europe. Fate decided to serve Darnley the same ending as Rizzio before he too could run away.

Darnley's behaviour after the birth of his son James changed little towards Mary. Having failed to get what he wanted through violence; Darnley's next tact was to blackmail his wife. Firstly, he convinced his father, the Earl of Lennox, to write to the queen claiming his son was a victim and was humiliated, as he had not been granted the just status of Crown Matrimonial. Lennox then implied that Darnley was threatening to abandon her and Prince James for Europe unless things changed, and he got what he wanted. Thankfully, Mary acted swiftly when she received this missive from her father-in-law and sought help from her privy council. Although her council was made up of men, many of whom disliked having a young woman as their monarch, especially a Catholic woman, they were still willing to support her in favour of her arrogant husband Darnley. This dislike of Darnley was due to him failing to prove himself worthy of trust or respect. Instead the counsellors felt he was humiliating Mary by threatening to leave her and his heir.

While the council was still holding its meeting, Darnley turned up at Holyroodhouse but refused to enter until the meeting had been concluded. Eventually, Mary enticed her husband, like a naughty child, to stop behaving badly. She convinced Darnley to come into the palace where he spent the evening within her personal apartments. During that night, she was able to, by fair or foul means, get her sulky, arrogant husband to consent to meet her counsellors the following morning in order to work through Darnley's grievances and complaints. The next day, Darnley met with the privy council where he proceeded to lie and refused to explain his behaviour or express any of his petty grievances with Mary or the members of council. He went on and denied ever wanting to leave for Europe to join his friends in their self-imposed exiles. He left the council meeting having conveyed the impression that he was both cooperative and responsible. As the letter had not been sent to Mary from Darnley but from the Earl of Lennox, the council was persuaded by his performance.

After meeting with the privy council, Darnley left Holyroodhouse and travelled towards Glasgow in the company of his father the Earl of Lennox. Once out of the reach of Mary and her counsellors in the Scottish village of Corstophine, Darnley wrote to Mary saying that he did still intend to leave, that he was angry at being snubbed and shunned by the leading men of the land and hurt by her lack of trust in him to hold any regal power. Both Mary and the counsellors had their evidence, and they agreed that Darnley would never hold a position of power in Scotland. The queen's husband was reaping what he had sown, and he had nobody but himself to blame for his lack of favour. Darnley arrived in Glasgow and proceeded to act like a king by hunting, fishing and revelling in Fife, Kinross and Loch Leven, and ignoring invites to accompany the queen to the assizes (where she would be present as the ceremonial head of the justice system) within the border area of Scotland.

It was during mid-October, while she was still on progress, that Mary became seriously ill. The queen's symptoms included fever, convulsions, loss of speech and the vomiting of blood. In order to recuperate, Mary found herself bed-bound at Jedburgh Castle. Despite being informed of his wife's illness, Darnley remained in Glasgow quite unconcerned. As her second husband was absent without leave, Mary summoned the man who would, within the year, become her third husband, James Hepburn, 4th Earl of Bothwell. He was part of the queen's council, and although a member of the aristocracy, he was notably rough in his manner and behaviour. At the time of Mary's request, Bothwell was seriously injured himself. He had been part of Mary's royal party on progress when he was involved in an altercation that led to him being stabbed.

The queen's association with Bothwell had started while she was still in France. He had arrived at the French court in the later part of 1560 and Mary had welcomed her countryman who must have charmed both Francois II and Mary sufficiently, as he was given 600 crowns as well as a position within the king's household as Gentleman of the King's Chamber. He did eventually return to Scotland but made two further journeys to the Parisian court, once in the spring of 1561 and again a few months later, in July, when he would help Mary arrange her to return to Scotland.

Gradually, Mary made a full recovery from her mysterious bout of illness and she and her royal party relocated to Craigmillar Castle in the later part of November. While staying at Craigmillar, the queen and her council met to discuss how to deal with her feckless husband, Darnley. The details of the discussions are unrecorded however rumour of them must have reached Darnley's ears as he decided to return to the refuge and safety of his parent's estates near Glasgow for the festive season. While travelling to the Lennox estates, Darnley also fell ill, with what is widely believed by historians to have been a flare-up of his reoccurring syphilis.

Mary spent that festive period of 1566 in Holyroodhouse away from her husband. In the new year, 1567, Mary requested that her husband return to Edinburgh to continue his recovery. Surprisingly, he did return and stayed in a part of Edinburgh known as Kirk o'Field. As he continued to recover, the queen visited him frequently. Whether this was an attempt at reconciliation or to give the impression to the people of Edinburgh that she and Darnley were on friendly terms, it is unclear. As January turned into to February, Darnley remained at Kirk o'Field and it would be the last place he would call home.

During the evening before Darnley's death, the queen was celebrating the nuptials of one of the members of her household, Bastian Pagez. He had come to Scotland with the widowed queen from her French household as a musician. After the merrymaking and celebrations had finished, Mary went to her private quarters within Holyroodhouse. Whether she knew about what would happen that coming night is still up for debate to this day. Early in the morning of 10 February, at around 2.00 am, there was a loud explosion heard from the direction of Kirk o'Field. The cause of the explosion was blamed on poorly stored barrels of gunpowder within the lodge's cellars. One member of staff within the household was killed but in the immediate aftermath of the explosion, no one could find the visiting Darnley.

The household staff searched, and Darnley was eventually found along with his personal valet, in a state of undress, stripped naked from the waist down and lying within an orchard that formed part of the Kirk o'Field estate. Darnley and his man servant had been killed by suffocation or strangulation and not as a result of the explosion from the gunpowder within the lodges cellars. This brings up so many questions: Was he running away from the lodge? Were he and his valet killed prior to the explosion or afterwards? We know that Darnley was bisexual, but at the time of the explosion were he and his servant actually engaged in something intimate? Were they already in the orchard at the time the gunpowder went off? If not, why were they found in the orchard? There are so many questions, the biggest being, had Mary ordered her husband to be killed at that meeting she held at Craigmillar Castle at the end of the previous year? Did she know it was going to happen? As well as who did it?

The haste in which of Darnley's funeral was arranged and carried out says much about what both Mary and her counsellors thought of her second husband. Due to his unpopularity and to avoid reprisals, he was buried at night, four days after the explosion, on St Valentine's Day after mass was celebrated in the chapel of Holyroodhouse. It would have done more for Mary's integrity if she had held a small state funeral and shown some element of mourning for her second husband. Mary was now a widow for the second time. This time, the death of her husband was scandalous and the consequences of his death and the events that would follow, would prompt Mary to leave Scotland and seek safety and refuge with her cousin Elizabeth.

During her last period of crisis when she needed to leave France and her mother-in-law, Mary had called upon the Earl of Bothwell to help arrange her passage back to Scotland. It is not surprising that at this new period of turmoil Mary sought out a friendly and reliable man to help her and she once again she chose Bothwell. The Protestant fraction of the council led by her half-brother, the Earl of Moray, had not only been able to remove the reckless Darnley, but now, scandal and rumour had started to damage Mary's reputation as well. This opened up an opportunity for Moray's allies on the privy council to manipulate, control and even potentially ruin the Queen of Scots. Rumours started to circulate that Mary had ordered Darnley's murder and the obvious person to accuse of this deadly deed was of course her closest ally - the Earl of Bothwell.

Not everyone was relieved to be free of 'the Darnley problem'. Chief of his mourners were his family, led by his father the 4th Earl of Lennox. Two months after Darnley's murder, on 12 April, the Earl of Bothwell was called in front of the queen's privy council under pressure from the Lennox clan and its supporters, to face charges of murder against the late Lord Darnley and his valet. Justice in the sixteenth century was often swift and rarely fair especially in treason and capital offence trials. The earl's hearing started at midday and was concluded that evening by 19.00 pm and the privy counsellors acquitted Bothwell of killing Darnley. Though, this didn't technically make him innocent, the important fact was that Bothwell could now not be legally accused and subsequently retried for the same crime again. Of course, this ambiguous outcome just adds fuel to the rumours and mythology surrounding this event in history and of Mary, Queen of Scots herself.

Elizabeth was kept well informed of the goings-on in Scotland and she and her advisors Walsingham and Cecil could see what was brewing. The scandalous death of Darnley was more than the messy personal life of Mary being exposed for the world to see; Elizabeth and her counsellors saw it as a weapon that could be used against the Scottish Queen politically. Elizabeth knew through her own experiences, that Mary, because of her gender and Catholicism, was particularly vulnerable in a post-reformation Scotland. Elizabeth had experienced similar scandals and had managed to survive both politically and literally by learning from her mother's mistakes and keeping away from trouble. Whether in an act of female solidarity and sisterly love or for selfish, political reasons, Elizabeth sent her cousin advice saying that she should distance herself from Bothwell and the scandal of her late husband's death. The National Archives have a translated transcript of the letter that was originally written in French:

> 'Madam, My ears have been so astounded and my heart so frightened to hear the horrible and abominable murder of your husband and my own cousin that I have scarcely spirit to write: yet I cannot conceal that I grieve more for you

than him. I should not do the office of a faithful cousin and friend, if I did not urge you to preserve your honour, rather than look through your fingers at revenge on those who have done you that pleasure as most people say. I counsel you so to take this matter to heart, that you may show the world what a noble princess and loyal woman you are. I write thus vehemently not that I doubt, but for affection' *(Elizabeth I to Mary Queen of Scots 24 Feburary 1567 ref: SP52/13f.17 National Archieves Kew)*

History however tells us that for whatever reason, Mary decided not to heed Elizabeth's sage advice. The two women did have an open rivalry, and Mary may well have resented Elizabeth's interference, or she might even have been naïve enough to think that just because Bothwell had been acquitted that he was no longer tainted with suspicion. The other possibility was that she was in love with Bothwell and blinded by emotion and that is why she chose to ignored the advice from Elizabeth. Regardless of her motivations, this was to be another poor decision made by Mary.

Astonishingly, Bothwell managed to go from suspected murderer to Mary's third husband in the space of mere weeks. How he became Mary's third and final husband is no less astonishing. It is also this last part of Mary's reign that is often the most fictionalised, romantised and scandalised. Moray wasted no time in taking advantage of Mary's now ruined reputation.

Bothwell may have been rougher in manner and language than the average Scottish aristocrat, but he was politically savvy. Days after his acquittal he brought leading men and clergy together for dinner at an Edinburgh inn known as the Ainsile Tavern. During this meal, Bothwell persuaded the men to put their names to a bond, that stated that Bothwell's trial had been fair, and that the outcome had been legal. He also managed to get the gathering to recommend him as Mary's next husband.

Armed with his bond, several days later, on the 24 April, Bothwell with a crew of eight hundred armed men, met up with the queen as she was travelling from Linlithgow Palace, back to Edinburgh fifteen miles away. He informed the queen that there was an angry mob waiting for her in Edinburgh and that for her own safety, she should accompany him to his castle, located in Dunbar. Mary decided to go to Dunbar with Bothwell but whether it was of her own free will or under duress we will never know. There is a myth surrounding these events that Bothwell kidnapped and imprisoned Mary and subsequently raped her, thus forcing her into marriage with him. However, Bothwell was armed with the bond signed by high ranking members of state and church, recommending him as Mary's next husband and Mary herself had twice turned to Bothwell for help - it is therefore more logical to conclude that Mary was more than a willing participant and followed Bothwell by her own accord. During this period, the pair were probably intimate. There was one last obstacle to Bothwell's plan - at the time of Darnley's death, the Earl of Bothwell was in fact married himself.

The earl had married Lady Jean Gordon during February 1566. Conveniently, the couple were granted a divorce in May 1567, on the grounds that Bothwell had been having an adulterous liaison with one of his wife's female servants. The divorce was finalised on 7 May, leaving Bothwell legally free to remarry, which he did eight days later, on 15 May 1567.

On 6 May, Mary and Bothwell issued their marriage ban to the Kirk of St Giles. Their ban or intention to marry had to be read as part of the sixteen century's canonical law requirement in Scotland and is still a requirement in some countries today. However, the Kirk refused to read it on the grounds that there were rumours circulating that the marriage was pending due to the abduction and subsequent rape of the queen. The following day, Mary wrote to St Giles' radical preacher, John Knox in order to reassure him that she was entering the marriage of her own free will. The Kirk had no choice and the ban was reluctantly read aloud by Knox's assistant, John Craig on 7 May. Four days later, Craig renewed his objections to the marriage in a public sermon at St Giles. Although this angered Bothwell, it did not stop the marriage from going ahead. On 14 May the marriage contract was signed, enabling Mary and Bothwell to get married the following day. On the morning of 15 May 1567, Mary Queen of Scots got married for the third and final time. The ceremony took place at the Holyroodhouse in a Protestant service – Bothwell was a Protestant, but Catholic Mary's decision might also have been an attempt to gain acceptance from her subjects and counsellors. It was a quiet affair. Mary's French family and connections spurned the ceremony in protest of the scandalous match. Although it was a private and dignified occasion, Mary still walked down the aisle in a style befitting her status as Queen of Scotland. Her gown was of black Italian velvet and richly decorated with detailed embroidery. It was only three short months and five days since her second husband, Darnley had been found half naked and strangled in an Edinburgh orchard. The short period of time between his death and her remarriage was both scandalous and undignified.

As Mary began her third marriage, her political enemies, the Confederate Lords, were meeting in the east coast city of Stirling, plotting how to rid themselves of their vain Catholic queen and make her infant son, Prince James, the new king.

This episode in history clearly shows the distinct differences in queenship between the two royal cousins Mary and Elizabeth. Elizabeth did try to advise her cousin after Darnley's death. Sadly, Mary allowed herself to get swept up in romantic drama, seeking the help of the most manipulative and scheming rescuer available to her, the Earl of Bothwell. Mary's sheltered, happy court childhood in France had not prepared her for life as queen, especially a queen of her fractious home country of Scotland. It is of course impossible to know if things would have been different had Mary dealt with the aftermath of Darnley's death by distancing herself from Bothwell. But it can be argued that her poor decisions and lack of judgement would affect the rest of her life.

1567: The Abdication of Mary Queen of Scots & her Escape to England

Sadly, Mary's third marriage was no happier than her second. It soon became apparent to the queen that Bothwell had manipulated her affections to rise to power. The French ambassador du Croc reported passionate arguments between the couple within the confines of their apartments within Holyroodhouse. Regardless of how miserable she was personally, when in public, Mary put on a great show of being happy and likewise Bothwell was respectful and gentlemanly towards Mary. However, the queen was not the only member of her court growing to dislike Bothwell.

Slowly, Mary's remaining lords were growing angry and frustrated at the increasing influence and power that Bothwell wielded as the queen's husband. Although Bothwell seems to have learnt from Darnley's mistakes and did not demand titles, he did manage to excise power within the council. One by one, the privy counsellors started to defect to the Confederate Lords who were still based in Stirling.

One of the first to defected was James Douglas, 4th Earl of Morton, who was an ambitious man. Morton's survival tactic was to migrate and support the most dynamic and influential courtiers of the moment and as they lost favour or influence, he moved on to the next rising star. A good example of this behaviour was when he was part of Darnley's clique and even played a role in the vicious murder of David Rizzio. But as soon as Darnley started to wane from influence, Morton defected to the lords who surrounded Bothwell. Again, once Bothwell stopped being influential and useful, Morton defected again, this time to the Confederate Lords, and in doing so, he made himself an enemy of Bothwell.

Mary and Bothwell left Holyroodhouse on 6 June and relocated the court to Borthwick Castle, about twelve miles from Edinburgh in the hope that this relocation would protect them from Moray and the hostile lords. Four days later, during the evening, the Confederate Lords approached the court at Borthwick Castle. Bothwell decided to escape, leaving his wife the queen, to take refuge in the castle battlements, where she shouted and cursed at the lords below like a common fishwife. With Bothwell gone, the lords retreated, to rethink their plan to attack the city of Edinburgh the next day.

Edinburgh had previously been loyal to Mary, however the following day, the people abandoned her. This was a great victory for the Confederate Lords. The first action they took was to call all able-bodied men to arms, using the pretence that Bothwell had put 'violent hands on the queen's person', 'having murdered the late king' and 'gathering together forces to murder the young prince'.

As Edinburgh was arming to take on Bothwell, Mary made a daring escape from Borthwick Castle dressed in men's clothes, riding hard through the night to Dunbar Castle arriving on the morning of 13 June. Bothwell, who had arrived at his castle first left Dunbar soon after Mary's arrival. He was leaving for an assignation within the border area of Scotland as he hoped he could rally more support there; but Bothwell was the only person to show up at the prearranged spot, Melrose. Unlike her husband, Mary was able to attract men to their cause, but the numbers were not as promising as she had expected.

On 15 June, exactly one month after they had married, Mary and Bothwell faced their foes at a place called Carberry Hill. Carberry Hill is situated roughly eight miles east of Edinburgh and is a wide, hilly plane of land surrounded by small towns and villages. Both the queen and the opposing lords followed each other around Carberry, neither side willing to strike first. The two sides were fairly evenly matched. If the confrontation had taken place earlier, Mary and Bothwell would have stood a better chance of winning the skirmish. Things were at a standstill and as the morning turned into a warm afternoon, Mary's men were hot and thirsty with a lack of access to drinking water. They were also impatient like all military men, who get frustrated waiting to fight.

In the early afternoon, the royal troops were issued strong beer and wine, a fatal error made by Mary's side. The frustrated and bored men over drank the strong alcoholic beverages and became drunk and further dehydrated. The men started to drift away, abandoning Mary and Bothwell. At 14.00 pm, a representative from the Confederate Lords came riding to the royal side, waving a white flag and asking to parlé. The lords had sent Kirkaldy of the Grange (William Kirkaldy was a leading member of the Scottish reformation movement) to deliver the message from the Lords. They wanted Mary to abandon Bothwell. If she was to do that, they would stand down their fighting men and be loyal to her. This was Mary's golden opportunity to get rid of the temperamental and violent Bothwell, and to attempt to re-establish her reign and power as the Queen of Scotland with all her influential lords. However, for reasons unknown, Mary stood by Bothwell. This decision made on 15 June 1567, would ultimately start Mary on the path to exile in Elizabeth's England.

Bothwell was angered and insulted by the lords' proposals and to avenge the disrespect that they had demonstrated publicly towards the queen and himself, he responded by offering to fight a nominated lord in a one-on-one duel to the death. Kirkcaldy returned with the royal party's reply and was promptly sent back by the lords to accept Bothwell's offer to duel. Bothwell only wanted to fight one man - his former friend and ally, Morton. After rejecting several other alternative candidates, the Confederate Lords were finally able to convince Morton to duel with Bothwell. Morton, who was older and less fit than Bothwell, and had good reason to be an unwilling opponent. Sixteenth century duelling etiquette allowed for each side to have a surrogate, who could fight in place of the original combatant. Morton's surrogate was Lord Lindsay who had willingly volunteered for the role as he had his own personal motive for wanting to fight Bothwell; he was related to the late Lord Darnley. But as Bothwell and Lindsay prepared to face each other to the death, Mary stepped in and called a halt to the duel. She knew that regardless of who won, neither side would be happy, and that violent fighting was no way to resolve a political problem. While the two sides negotiated, the afternoon had worn on and more of the royal troops had started to desert or were too inebriated to fight. Mary had understood that their chance had been lost and she decided to end this stand-off on her terms, and she surrendered to the Confederate Lords on the condition that Bothwell was allowed to escape. In return, she would go with them to Edinburgh. The Confederate Lords had won the first battle for the throne of Scotland and were on their way to replacing the Queen of Scotland with her infant son, James.

If Mary had expected the Confederate Lords to treat her with the respect and dignity expected of her title of queen, then she was very swiftly to be disappointed yet again. Before the party had even made the short journey back to Edinburgh, Mary had been catcalled, jeered and mocked by the lords. These insults were followed up with calls to, 'Burn the whore'. As if being called a whore was not humiliating enough, upon returning to her capital city, the Confederate Lords did not bring her to one of her royal homes, but she was expected to lodge in one of the city administrator's homes close to St Giles Kirk and the market cross. The lords had deceived and misled Mary as convincingly as both Darnley and Bothwell had done and consequently, she found herself under house-arrest and at their mercy.

The true intentions of the lords became apparent the following day on, 16 June, when they had a meeting with the French ambassador, du Croc. The purpose of this tryst was to investigate how Mary's old allies would react if she were to be put aside as monarch in favour of her infant son, Prince James. Catherine de Medici, who was still regent for her son, Charles IX of France, was still no friend to her one-time daughter-in-law. The only reason that the French would consider interfering is if England and Elizabeth were to come to Mary's aid, using *military* means. France would not allow her old enemy the 'god damns' to interfere with Scottish politics.

Later in the afternoon of the 16 June, the lords took Mary, under escort, to Holyroodhouse. The lord in charge of her was Morton and ahead of them in a procession to Holyroodhouse, were men carrying the heraldic banner of the once despised and loathed Darnley. Mary had to endure jeers and taunts from her subjects, with some calling her a murderess and a whore and demanding her death. Upon arrival at Holyroodhouse, Mary had little time to get settled in, as the plan was to move her again that evening to Lochleven during the hours of darkness. Mary would never see Edinburgh or Holyrood house again.

Lochleven was a cruel place to imprison Mary and not just because of its isolated location. The Laird of Lochleven was Sir William Douglas and he and his mother both inhabited the loch fortress. Douglas's mother was Lady Margret Erskine, who had been Mary's late father's mistress and she was also the mother of Mary's step-brother, the Earl of Moray. What made things even more awkward was that Lady Margaret was very outspoken about her relationship with James V. She also claimed that she and the late king had been more than lovers and that they had been in fact married making Mary's step-brother Moray, who was 11 years her senior, the rightful King of Scotland in her opinion. As if that was not uncomfortable enough, one of Douglas's sisters was married to Lord Lindsay, the Confederate Lord who had volunteered to fight Bothwell for Morton and had been related to Darnley. Poor Mary, the harsh and unfriendly conditions of her captivity in the fortress in Lochleven caused her both physical and mental harm that would intensify in mid-July, when it is said that she miscarried a double pregnancy, children she claimed to have been Bothwell's.

Then on 24 July, while she was still recovering from her lost pregnancy, Mary's quarters were descended on by a band of the Confederate Lords who intended to manipulate the queen while she was still weak. They presented her with abdication papers, proposing that she step down in favour of her infant son James, who would have his half-uncle Moray act as his regent until he was of age. They also proposed that the lords should rule until little James was crowned at his coronation and Moray arrived back in Scotland from his self-imposed exile in France.

Mary's initial reaction was of course to refuse the lords' demands. However, the ruthless and bullying Lindsay threatened Mary with violence and death if she refused to sign the documents. Reluctantly and knowing that she had been beaten, Mary signed her crown over to her infant son, Prince James. On 29 July, four days after his mother abdicated, James was crowned in the city of Stirling. The Confederate Lords had won the last battle in the struggle for power and the Scottish throne.

It is worth noting that when Elizabeth heard of Mary's predicament and of her forced abdication, she was deeply angered at the behaviour of the Confederate Lords. Elizabeth held a firm belief in the ideology of the divine right of sovereigns and felt that the lords had violated this very sacred position held by monarchs. Elizabeth offered to aid her cousin against her captors, but between Cecil and the Confederate Lords, Mary never knew of Elizabeth's offer of help. Elizabeth it seems was only willing to help Mary if she was to remain in Scotland.

The castle fortress of Lochleven became Mary's home for the next ten months. During that period, she was able to have a small household of servants and she took this time to recuperate physically and mentally from her experiences since the death of Darnley. She filled her days with sewing, playing cards and dancing. She may have given the laird the impression she was accepting her fate and settling into life under house-arrest, but she was in fact biding her time and making the best of a bad situation. Little did she know that it would be practice for the later years of her life in England.

During those those months at Lochleven, Mary made quite an impression on George Douglas - William Douglas's younger brother. He ended up falling hopelessly and passionately in love with Mary, and although there was never a relationship between the two, Mary was able to use his affections to help her escape the prison of Lochleven. As soon as George's affections for Mary became obvious to the rest of the family he was banished from the castle. This did not stop the pair, who were still able to communicate through members of Mary's household, from plotting and they managed to mastermind a plot to help Mary escape from Lochleven and Scotland.

The 2 May was part of the May Day celebrations and the Douglas family had a day out enjoying the spring festivities. George Douglas and Mary had managed to recruit a member of William Douglas's household to help them in their scheme. The page was known as Little Willie. His first task was to vandalise and scupper all but one of the boats moored at Lochleven. Willie's next assignment was more trickery as he had to acquire the key to Lochleven's entrance while the family sat down to enjoy their supper. Once these tasks were completed, he needed to signal to Mary that he done what was required. Mary was then to go down to the castle courtyard dressed in one of her serving women's clothes and from there, Willie and Mary were to lock the castle gates and row across the loch to the waiting party of men headed by George Douglas, who had a horse ready for Mary.

The plan went without a hitch and with no time to waste, Mary and George Douglas rode hard and fast away from Lochleven across the landscape of Fife to the Firth of Forth. Now with enough distance between Mary and Lochleven she was able to rest for the night at a property that belonged to one of her serving women, Mary Seton. Over the next ten days, Mary was able to rally a sizeable army to help her. On the 13 May, Mary's troops faced the Confederate Lords fronted by Moray in what became known as the Battle of Langside. Although Mary's army is reported to have been larger than that of her enemies, she was defeated after forty-five minutes of fighting. Mary had to flee the site of battle and abandon her loyal troops, so that she could make it to Dumfries. The following night, she retreated to the Cistercian abbey of Dundrennan in Galloway, where she would spend her last night on

Scottish soil. Before retiring for the night in her monastic refuge, Mary wrote to Elizabeth begging her for help and assistance. Within the correspondence Mary enclosed the diamond ring that Elizabeth had sent Mary in friendship, five years earlier.

The following day, on 16 May, Mary crossed the Solway Forth and arrived in Northern England. Little did she know that she was jumping out of the pan and into the fire. Meanwhile, as Mary was heading for what she thought was the sanctuary of Elizabeth's England, Elizabeth was busy admiring her newest jewel, a pearl that the Scottish lords had sold to Elizabeth from Mary's treasury at Holyroodhouse. As much as Elizabeth had been shocked and angered by Mary's treatment as a sister queen, it seems Elizabeth was only willing to help Mary at a distance and only if it benefitted Cecil and Walshingham's plans. Mary's arrival would dominate and affect Elizabeth's reign for the next seventeen years; causing religious struggles in England that had not been seen since 'Bloody' Mary Tudor's reign. The former Scottish queen's presence would not only affect domestic policies but also England's relations with the rest of Catholic Europe, too.

1569: The Northern Rebellion

Traditionally the north of England had remained loyal to the Catholic faith after the English reformation under Henry VIII, probably helped by the fact that it was so far from the influential reformist campaigners based in the capital. Even during Henry's own reign, the north had risen up in York under the leadership of Robert Aske who had attempted to bring England back to Rome during the Pilgrimage of Grace in 1536.

Initially, in the early part of Elizabeth's reign at least, the new queen had attempted to achieve a religious tolerance so that both Catholics and Protestants could commune with God as they wished. Cecil and Walsingham felt that this was not a prudent course to resume after the unexpected arrival of Mary Queen of Scots in the north of England as her presence made the issue of religion, both politically and personally dangerous to Elizabeth's reign and wellbeing.

Despite the many stresses that she had endured over the years, Mary Queen of Scots was still beautiful and her fine looks along with her scandalous and intoxicating allure made Mary unsurprisingly attractive, not just to men but also to the marginalised Catholics. Lords who had not previously questioned the suitability of Elizabeth as their queen suddenly found a Catholic contender living under house arrest in the north of England. Elizabeth may have been Henry's daughter and had been named her late sister's successor, but she still had her illegitimate status. These factors would surely be enough to plant the seed of doubt into the minds of many good Catholic lords in the north, over the question of Elizabeth's right to the crown.

In comparison, Mary was not only legitimate, but she had been the Queen of Scotland practically since birth, and she had briefly been the Queen of France. In addition, she had an heir in Prince James which would make the uncertain issue of succession less complex than in Elizabeth's case. Mary also had a claim to the English throne in her own right through her linage via Margret Tudor; Elizabeth and Mary were cousins, after all and it is interesting to think think what may have happened had Mary Queen of Scots not been in France at the time of Mary Tudor's last illness, 'Bloody' Mary might well have nominated the Scottish Queen as her successor instead of her Protestant step-sister Elizabeth. Of course, we will never know the answer to that one, but it is enough to know that it may have been a possibility had circumstances been different.

It is little wonder then that both William Cecil and Sir Francis Walsingham, Elizabeth's chief ministers, who were both staunch Protestants, became anxious at the arrival of Mary in the Catholic north of England. The English nobility was after all notorious for its rivalries and battles for power. Mary's presence offered them a legitimate justification, in the name of faith, to seek positions of influence.

In 1569, Cecil and Walsingham's worst nightmare became a temporary reality. Mary had attracted the attentions of the Catholic northern nobility and they were unhappy that she was under house arrest. The first solution that the northern lords thought of to help Mary was to arrange a marriage for her with Thomas Howard, Duke of Norfolk. While the queen pondered the problem of Mary in London with the privy council, the northern lords were trying to figure out how best to use Mary to help them to re-establish Catholicism and make Mary Stuart, the Queen of England, thereby replacing Elizabeth.

The two lords that led what became known as the Northern Rebellion or The Rising of the North were Charles Neville, 6th Earl of Westmorland and Thomas Percy, 7th Earl of Northumberland. Another important northern noble family that took part in the rising and supported the earl's cause was the Nortons, who were led by Richard Norton better known as 'Old Norton' and several of his sons. Old Norton had taken part in the Pilgrimage of Grace under the reign of Henry VIII and was therefore fully committed to reinforcing the Catholic doctrine upon the English. The rebel earls and their supporters were betrayed by Leonard Dacre, who had initially encouraged the rebellion before thinking better of his involvement and giving their names to the queen and her council. The earls had to strike before the queen's men made it up north to quash them or give up without trying.

The first stage of their strategic plan was to capture the city of Durham and hold it as the rebels had done with York in the Pilgrimage of Grace.

When they entered the city, the rebels' first action was to remove the Protestant prayer books and bibles from the cathedral to show the citizens of Durham what they were there to fight for. On 30 November 1569, Catholic mass was celebrated in Latin within the cathedral for the first time since Mary Tudor's death.

The rebels made Durham their base for the next week and half before moving on and re-establishing the Latin mass and ceremonies in Ripon, Richmond (Yorkshire) and Darlington. Elizabeth sent Walter Devereux, 1st Earl of Essex (father of the 2nd Earl of Essex, Robert Devereux, who would raise a rebellion against the aged queen in 1601) up north to quash the rebellion. However, his troops were no match for the growing rebel numbers. Essex wrote to the queen to say he needed more men to defeat the insurgents. Unsure of Essex's loyalty, the queen dispatched a second man, Sir Ralph Sadler to verify Essex's claims and to check his loyalty to Elizabeth. Sadler wrote back to London confirming the rebel numbers and Essex's trustworthiness.

The next target that the rebels intended to take siege of was the city of York, as it was, and still is today, the second most important bishopric within the Church of England. For this crusading Catholic insurrection to take and keep hold of York was strategically important and the episcopacy would be a great triumph and morale booster for their cause. But this was not to be, the rebels discovered that York was where Elizabeth's men had gathered to hopefully defeat them. The rebels did not want to fight them within the city as innocent souls could have been harmed and fighting conditions were difficult due to the narrow side streets. So instead, they made their way to Clifford Moor. Here they waited until Essex and the queen's men choose to challenge their cause.

The extra men that a frustrated Essex and Sadler needed arrived on 13 December in the city of York. The queen's force had been joined by Ambrose Dudley, Earl of Warwick and Edward Clinton, Earl of Lincoln. This increase in royal numbers did not go unnoticed by the rebels, who in turn moved away from the royal forces and headed further north. In a last-ditch attempt to regroup and find a base, the rebels made their way to Leonard Dacre, the man who had disowned them and their cause to the queen. Dacre grudgingly gave shelter, but it was at this point the rebels realised that they had no chance of winning and decided to disband. Being so close to the Scottish border, many of the rebels hoped to find sanctuary in Scotland, out of reach of Elizabeth's men. Many were unlucky, getting caught or killed in their desperate attempts to cross the border. Amongst those caught were gentlemen Robert Pennyman of Stokesley, Thomas Bishop of Pocklington, Simon Digby of Aiskew and John Fulthorpe of Islebeck. These men were brought to York where they were held until parliament passed judgement and had sentenced them. They suffered traitors' deaths, being hung, drawn and quartered so that their bodies could be displayed, to remind the people of York of the consequences of rising up against the queen.

Dacre's last act of giving his former allies a brief place of shelter did not go unnoticed by the queen. Elizabeth expected full loyalty and by helping the rebels at the end, Dacre had not only committed treason but double-crossed Elizabeth too. The queen's response was to send Lord Hudson to capture him as a traitor. Dacre faced the queens' men at Gelt's Bridge in Cumbria in a skirmish that would become known locally as the Dacre Raid. Dacre's side, comprising of many women, was crushed while the cowardly Dacre was able to escape capture, first fleeing to Scotland and then to Flanders where he lived the rest of his life in exile away from justice and the reach of Elizabeth. He died in Europe six years later in 1575.

The first leader of the rebellion, the Earl of Northumberland, managed to escape over the Scottish border, however, that was where his luck ran out. He was captured by Mary Queen of Scots' enemy, step-brother and then regent of Scotland, Moray. The regent held him, ironically, on the same island castle that he'd kept Mary, Lochleven. Moray kept Northumberland there for three years before he surrendered him to the English in 1572 and he was brought to York to face his death. Unlike the men executed three years before him, Northumberland was spared the long and painful death of being hung, drawn and quartered, but was instead led to a scaffold to be beheaded. His head was displayed as per tradition and the rest of his remains were buried without service in a local church, St Crux. Northumberland's co-conspirator and leader, Lord Westmorland was luckier as he was able to escape to Europe and resided in Spanish Flanders where he was given a small pension from the Spanish. As well as the nobility involved in the rebellion, it is thought that sixty-six other men were convicted and executed for their part in the uprising.

The last notable and relevant person to mention is Thomas Howard, Duke of Norfolk. Although it seems he supported the cause and he was put forward as a suitable husband for Mary Queen of Scots, there was no solid proof that he was actually involved in the plotting or helped the northern rebels. But his tenuous connection to the rebellion was enough to earn him nine months in the Tower of London at Elizabeth's pleasure. He initially got involved with the plot, as he saw it as an opportunity to prove himself, as he felt that his cousin, Elizabeth, did not trust or value him within her council. These feelings of resentment towards Elizabeth were exaggerated after his time in The Tower and this did not deter him from committing treason in the future; so much so that he would later play a role in the Ridolfi Plot. This was another scheme, attempting to replace Elizabeth I with Mary Queen of Scots.

The rebellion affected Elizabeth as it was the prompt that caused Pope Pius V to issue a papal bull against the English Queen and to excommunicate her the following year in 1570. In turn, this would prompt Mary Stuart to become central to several other plots to depose Elizabeth, in favour of her Catholic cousin.

It is fair to say that Elizabeth had learnt a lot from how from her father had dealt with the rebels who had taken part in the Pilgrimage of Grace during his reign. Elizabeth was swifter with her punishment but like her father before her, she had the traitors executed within their home cities to remind the locals that although they were far from London, Elizabeth's justice was still able to reach that far north.

1570: The Excommunication from Rome

As well as being a religious leader and God's Catholic representative on earth, the pope was then as he is now, also the leader of the small city state of the Vatican. With this aspect of his role, the pope was therefore more than a spiritual teacher, he was a political leader to the world's Catholics as well. This also meant that Catholics, then and now, weren't only led and governed by their nations' head of states, but also by the pope. This was not particularly problematic if Catholics lived in a Catholic country, as in theory, the state and the church would be ruling in harmony. But Catholics living in England were ruled by Elizabeth, who was a committed Protestant within the Anglican communion. Although she had been tolerant of her Catholic subjects' right to pray as they wished, they still felt marginalised.

The pope at the beginning of Elizabeth's reign was the elderly Paul IV. He was reluctant to excommunicate Elizabeth due to her Anglicanism upon her succession to the throne. This was probably because Elizabeth had set out a more religiously tolerant rule than her brother Edward VI had done. He may have also hoped that Elizabeth would continue with her step-sister's counter-reformation and he planned to wait and see how her reign would progress before taking action. But popes like monarchs die and Paul IV died in the first summer of Elizabeth's reign on 18 August 1559. He was succeeded by Pope Pius IV. His time as the pope was relatively short and like his predecessor, he was reluctant to act against Elizabeth despite her Protestant faith. At the end of 1565 at 66-years-old, Pius IV died, leaving the throne of St Peter's vacant until a new Bishop of Rome was elected in early 1566. The new pope, Pius V, was elected by the cardinal conclave on 7 January 1566. Initially, for the first few years of his incumbency, Pope Pius V left Elizabeth alone, but this changed when Elizabeth imprisoned, rather than helped her Catholic cousin, Mary Stuart, Queen of Scots. Elizabeth also further angered the

Vatican when she quashed the Northern Rising in 1569. Pius V saw this as Elizabeth persecuting English Catholics and he was not going to let her get away with it.

On 27 April 1570, Pope Pius V issued a papal bull against Elizabeth the 'heretic'. He used her illegitimate status as a weapon to discredit her and called her an usurper of the English throne stating:

> 'Among others, Elizabeth, the pretended queen of England and the servant of crime, has assisted in this, with whom as in a sanctuary the most pernicious of all have found refuge. This very woman, having seized the crown and monstrously usurped the place of supreme head of the Church in all England together with the chief authority and jurisdiction belonging to it, has once again reduced this same kingdom- which had already been restored to the Catholic faith and to good fruits- to a miserable ruin.' *(Papal Bull issued against Queen Elizabeth, 27 April 1570)*

These were damning words from the head of the Catholic church. The rest of the papal bull and excommunication against Elizabeth was literally a cry to battle to all Catholics, both English and European stating that deposing of or even killing Elizabeth was a good Catholic act and would not be considered a mortal sin. With religious tensions still running high after the Northern Rebellion, and despite Elizabeth's attempts at toleration, politically this was the last eventuality that Elizabeth needed. Although this was a trying time in her reign, it was a great opportunity for her Protestant counsellors, specifically Walshingham and Cecil, to manipulate circumstances and help them to find a way to get rid of the dangerous problem that was Mary Stuart Queen of Scots.

The consequences of this papal bull and excommunication reached further than Elizabeth's lifetime. Future monarchs, Charles I and his son eldest son, Charles II both struggled with religious tolerance during their reigns. These ecumenical struggles would ultimately play a role in how an anointed King of England, ended up being executed, and his eldest son, Charles II delaying his conversion to Rome until he was on his deathbed. The consequences even affected Charles I's younger son, James II as he was forced to abdicate and go into exile for his Catholic convictions while King of England.

The excommunication and papal bull did not just give Catholics within England the green light to try and depose of Elizabeth, but they also encouraged the Catholic superpowers of Europe to do the same. The biggest of these threats came from Elizabeth's one-time brother-in-law, Philip II of Spain. He was still bitter about Elizabeth's rebuff at the beginning of her reign and his inability to manipulate her in Spain's favour. As well as being the King of Spain, Philip also held the following titles: King of Naples, Sardinia, Sicily, Portugal and the Algarves, Lord of the Netherlands, Margave of Namur, Duke of Lothier, Milan, Brabant, Limburg, Guelders, Count of Charolias, Flanders, Hainaut, Artois, Holland, Zeeland, Zutphen and Count Palatine of Burgundy. As a member of the powerful Hapsburg royal house, he was well connected to Charles V who was the Holy Roman Emperor of Europe. Philip felt he had a God-given right to be a defender of the Catholic faith, as all monarchs of the sixteenth century did, at a time when Europe's kings and queens believed in the divine rights of sovereigns.

The other potentially problematic Catholic super-power on the continent, after the issuing of the papal bull, was France. England and France had always had a difficult relationship politically. Should the delicate good relations of 1570 get strained and these tensions rise to the surface again, then France, as a Catholic power, would have a ready-made excuse to attack England. At the time of the excommunication, Mary, Queen of Scots' former mother-in-law, Catherine de Medici was still alive. Catherine had been glad when Mary had returned to Scotland after her eldest son Francis I's death. As long as Catherine remained influential within the French court, it was unlikely that the French would support Mary's potential claim to the English crown; it suited Catherine de Medici to have Mary under house arrest. Thankfully, for England and Elizabeth, France also had a chequered relationship with her Catholic neighbour, Spain. Had these two powerful Catholic states been on better diplomatic terms, Elizabeth would have had to fear a mighty united Catholic superpower from these two nations.

1571: The Ridolfi Plot

With the failure of the Northern Rebellion and the subsequent issue of the papal bull, Catholics in both England and Europe began to think that Mary Stuart rather than Elizabeth Tudor should be the rightful Queen of England; and it was this way of thinking that led to the Ridolfi Plot.

The plot took its name from one of the major planners in the conspiracy - a renaissance banker from the city state of Florence called Robert Ridolfi. Ridolfi's family was made up of influential Florentine bankers and through his work, Ridolfi travelled throughout Europe including England. In around 1555, he decided to make the busy sixteenth century commercial metropolis of London as his new base. During this time, he met many powerful nobles and important people including the then Lady Elizabeth's secretary, William Cecil. As he arrived during Mary Tudor's reign, Ridolfi's Catholic faith wasn't an issue, and he made friends and acquaintances with many of the leading Catholics in England at the time. Much of Ridolfi's work still brought him to mainland Europe, and he would often carry messages and letters for his friends across the channel.

With the death of Mary and the start of the reign of Elizabeth, not much changed to start with for the Catholics living in England, this was because Elizabeth was at first, unwilling to impose one Christian denomination over another. With the arrival and house arrest of the Queen of Scots, Catholics started to feel threatened and to fear similar treatment to the fallen Queen of Scots. When the Northern Rebellion failed, despite the harsh punishments and retributions carried out across the north of England, many of England's leading Catholics grew more resentful and they turned to an obliging Ridolfi to help them recruit European assistance.

Ridolfi's role in the conspiracy that would bear his name was to be a convenient and discreet messenger to Elizabeth's arch nemesis',

Philip II of Spain, the Vatican and Fernando Alvarez de Toledo, Duke of Alba, who had armed men at his behest as well as easy access to England via the North Sea from the Dutch coast.

The remaining lords from the Northern Rebellion kept to the goals of their original plan. They wanted to release Mary and depose Elizabeth so that the former Queen of Scotland could become Queen of England. They also still hoped that Mary would marry the ambitious Duke of Norfolk, Thomas Howard, who also happened to be Elizabeth's second cousin. Although it is said that Norfolk told Ridolfi that he was a Catholic, he was curiously a patron of the Protestant chronicler, John Foxe too. He could of course have been one of the many Englishmen who changed their religious convictions to stay safe. But Norfolk's association with Foxe was strange all the same, given the aims of this conspiracy.

Another of the leaders was John Lesley, who was the Bishop of Ross. Those with religious careers must have felt especially unsettled with the swift religious changes that happened during the reigns of Henry VIII's three children. Bishops were men of influence and power. As well as their religious obligations many bishops were political too, and so it is easy to see why the Bishop of Ross may have felt compelled to act and to become involved with this treasonous plot. The Bishop of Ross would have been even more encouraged, personally and morally after the publication of the pope's bull against Elizabeth.

Philip II's man on the spot, was his ambassador to England and another of the plotters, Don Guerau de Espes del Valle. He had what he believed to be a legitimate cause to write to Philip II. He'd had a previous connection with Fernando Alvarez de Toledo, the Duke of Alba, during an uprising within the Spanish territories of Flanders, known as the Geuzens' Revolt of 1568. During this episode the two men had sought Elizabeth's help and English naval protection only for the queen's fleet to raid them after the Spanish ships had arrived safely in their territories within Flanders.

The last important conspirator was Mary, Queen of Scots herself. She was implicated by association with the plot but was not directly involved. She was the one who if the plot was successful would replace the deposed, and most likely assassinated Elizabeth, as queen. The plan was that Mary would then marry Norfolk and go on to reinstate the Catholic faith in England. However, her involvement was little more than knowledge of the plan and giving encouragement to the men acting to free her. This was not enough for Walsingham or Cecil to convict her of treason.

The treacherous plan became known to the Elizabethan court through several means. Elizabeth had never trusted Don Guerau de Espes del Valle after his involvement with the Geuzens' Revolt in 1568. The ever vigilant Walshingham, Elizabeth's bloodhound of a spymaster, felt similarly, and deployed a double agent, the naval admiral John Hawkins, to befriend the diplomat. In early 1571, the double agent managed to extract details of the plot from Guerau de Espes, putting the intelligence network on high alert. With suspicion at high levels, a papal agent named Charles Baille, who also had close ties with Mary Queen of Scots, was searched at Dover. It was discovered that he was carrying letters written in code. The poor man was brought to the Tower of London, interrogated and racked for the details of the decipher code.

The biggest breakthrough came in late summer of 1571, due to a misjudgment of trust made by two of the Duke of Norfolk's employees, William Barker and Robert Hingford. Instead of delivering a package of gold themselves, they decided to employ a certain Thomas Browne to take what they were told was silver, to one of Norfolk's associates. Barker and Hingford should have thought this deception through, as the weight of the package given to Browne was far heavier than the weight of silver. Curiosity got the better of Browne and he opened the parcel. Inside he found incriminating correspondence and a substantial sum of gold. Browne had two options: deliver it anyway and hope that his role in whatever was going on would be forgotten, or to tell someone at court. Wisely, Browne chose the latter, and made contact with Cecil.

Acting on this information, Cecil and Walsingham raided the Duke of Norfolk's property, his staff were arrested and viciously interviewed for information. The results of the search made upon the duke's home were fruitful as the searchers found a cipher for the letters they had found at Dover. The game was up. But Norfolk was still unaware of how much trouble he was in, at least for the time being, and he continued to deny any involvement with the plot. His arrest warrant was dispatched on 7 September 1571 which then saw him being brought to the Tower of London. Assessing his options, Norfolk quickly changed his story and decided it was better to admit involvement and to downplay his role in the affair. Norfolk did not know that Cecil and Walsingham had all the evidence they needed to charge him with high treason. His staff were not as loyal as he thought they would be, and the evidence they gave along with the letters that he thought had been destroyed all helped to seal his conviction.

The duke was tried for high treason during January 1572. Although there was little need for a trial, with the evidence that the privy council had gathered, parliament could have declared him guilty through an act of attainer. The trial was little more than a show-trial and he was inevitably found guilty. Despite getting the guilty verdict they required, Cecil and Walsingham would have to wait for the final fall of the axe as Elizabeth struggled to sign his death warrant. In total, Elizabeth signed and destroyed the warrant four times. The feeling of immense guilt over executing a member of her Boleyn family haunted her so much that on one occasion she used her royal pardon at 2.00 am on the day before he was due to be executed. Eventually, Cecil and Walshigham finally got their wish, and Norfolk went to the scaffold at Tower Hill on 2 June 1572. This episode solidified Walshingham and Cecil's mistrust of Mary Queen of Scots. It also indicated how Elizabeth may react to the prospect of having to sign the death warrant of her cousin and fellow anointed queen.

While reading the details of this chapter from Elizabeth's reign, and especially her reaction to the execution of the Duke of Norfolk, it is clear that the ghosts of her mother's death and possibly those of Catherine Howard and Lady Jane Grey pricked Elizabeth's conscience. She was reluctant to act as her father and later her step-sister had done, and she disliked the prospect of being perceived as an unmerciful queen. It was hard for her to strike a balance between compassion and safe guarding England's national security. But Norfolk had already been implicated in rebellion, and this had not deterred him from plotting again. Sadly, Mary Queen of Scots, did not learn from his fateful error.

1572: The St Bartholomew's Day Massacre

One of the biggest events that occurred during Elizabeth's reign didn't even happen on English soil. The St Bartholomew's Day Massacre took place in Paris and was witnessed by one of her most influential advisors, Sir Francis Walsingham. Walsingham held the position of Elizabeth's spymaster general and went on to develop anti-Catholic legal policies to protect his Protestant queen from continental Catholic threats partly as a result of the massacre.

Sir Francis Walsingham came from an aristocratic English family based in Kent. His kinsmen were some of the country's earliest reformers, and after receiving a humanist education, Francis went to Cambridge University, where he graduated with a law degree. Shortly after his graduation, Walsingham went into self-imposed exile during the Catholic reign of Elizabeth's sister Mary, taking refuge with other English Protestants exiles in Switzerland, only returning after Mary's death in late 1558. With Elizabeth now on the throne, Walsingham and the other exiles felt it was safe for them to return home.

Upon his return, Walsingham decided to make a career in politics and became MP for Bossiney in Cornwall, then Lyme Regis in Dorset and Banbury in Oxfordshire. This change of direction brought him to the attention of those in power. Once within the Tudor court, Walsingham elevated himself and his family both politically and socially.

As a committed reformist, Sir Francis wanted to make connections with the French Calvinist sect, known as the Huguenots, and would eventually become Elizabeth's ambassador in Paris. It was during this ambassadorship that Walsingham became caught up in the horrific events of the St Bartholomew's Day Massacre in 1572.

The religious reformation on mainland Europe had rocked the Catholic Church and divided the continent into two sides; Catholic and traditional versus modern and Protestant. The Protestant reform movement was started by a monk called Martin Luther who pinned his 95 Theses (a list of reforms attacking what he considered to be corrupt aspects of the Catholic doctrine) to his parish church in Wittenberg, Germany on 31 October 1517. His theories led other theological thinkers into considering the role of the Catholic church and a few agreed with Luther that the Catholic doctrine was seriously flawed. Not all the reformers agreed with all aspects of Luther's reasoning. Other small Protestant sects splintered off, creating new Protestant churches and amongst these new theologies were the Calvinists.

The theologian John Calvin (10 July 1509-27 May 1564) was a French reformer who like Martin Luther disliked the traditional Catholic doctrine. However, Calvin did not agree with all of Luther's reforms. Calvin became disillusioned with the Catholic Church around 1530; due to religious tensions within his native France. This caused him to migrate to the more tolerant city of Geneva in Switzerland. In 1555, Calvin offered refuge to English Protestants fleeing England under the reign of Mary I and they became known as the Meridian Exiles. The most ardent followers of Calvin were the French Huguenots. The Huguenots were primarily comprised of the merchant classes, who were French craftsmen and women primarily working within the weaving trade, living in the areas of France that bordered with Germany, such as the Alsace, Lorraine and Bourgogne-Franche-Comte. A decade before the massacre in Paris, it was estimated that the number of practising Huguenots within France was approximately two million faithful souls.

Local tensions between Catholics and Protestants grew and by 1562, these tensions had erupted into a religious civil war known as the French Wars of Religion, which lasted from 1562 to 1598. It was during this civil conflict that the Massacre of St Bartholomew's Day took place and inadvertently affected the foreign and domestic religious policy of the mid to late reign of Elizabeth I.

It is thought that the king's mother and queen regent of France at the time of the St Bartholomew's day Massacre, Catherine de Medici, actively encouraged Catholics to persecute and attack the Huguenot Calvinist minority. The massacre took place during the marriage of Catherine's daughter, Marguerite de Valois to the Protestant Henri III of Navarre. The marriage was an attempt at bringing both sides of the thirty-year religious civil war to a close, in the same way that Henry VII of England's marriage to Elizabeth of York, ended the civil unrest in England known as the War of the Roses.

The marriage took place in Paris, on 18 August 1572. The religious tensions of the ongoing civil war were brought to Paris with Henri III's relatives and entourage who were all Protestant. Tensions between the two sides of the divide grew, particularly after an attempt to murder the Huguenots' military leader, Gaspard de Coligny several days beforehand. Just days prior to the massacre, the Catholic Parisians attempted to score points against the Huguenots. Admiral De Coligny, was in Paris at the time to finish the delicate negotiations of the fragile treaty with Charles XI. After one of these treaty talks, being held at the Louvre, the admiral was shot as he was making his way back to his accommodation. The bullet hit him but failed to kill him. The goal of the assassination attempt had still been achieved, and the fragile peace was broken; the religious tensions that had been simmering for days finally turned into bloody chaos and violence. This violence spread into the rest of the city and death came to the streets of Paris on the evening of 23 August and into the following day.

The king, Charles IX, who was just 22 at the time, was shocked to hear of the attempt on Admiral De Coligny's life and went to visit him to reassure the wounded admiral that the attack on him would not go unpunished. Unfortunately, the Protestants were impatient and wanted vengeance for the attack on Admiral De Coligny sooner rather than later. They decided to force their way into the royal palace of the Louvre, where the queen regent was taking her evening meal and demanded that there was justice and punishment for the attack on their leader. This was not a wise move as unlike her son, the king, Catherine had no sympathy for the Huguenot cause.

A crisis meeting was called after the Huguenots had interrupted Catherine de Medici's supper, and if there was ever any proof of what happened during these discussions between the queen regent and her son the king, there is no longer any evidence available. Some historians believe that Catherine de Medici coerced Charles into agreeing to kill the remaining leadership of the Huguenot cause, so that it would be easier to quash any potential trouble within Paris. Other historians are less inclined to believe that the king agreed to such an action, willingly or under pressure from his mother. Either way, the result of that meeting remains unknown, and the bloody outcome was the same. In the time since Admiral De Coligny's attack, four thousand Huguenots had gathered outside the city walls, ready to take justice for their leader into their own hands. The delicate peace brought about by the marriage of Henri III of Navarre and Margritette de Valois looked like it would fail.

Paris went into lockdown. Orders were issued to the Swiss Guard, who at this time also protected the royal courts on continental Europe, as well as the pope in the Vatican, to find and execute all the Huguenot leaders. During the night, Paris barricaded herself and the city prepared for the worst. As with all military plans, there was an agreed signal to start the search and attack; that signal was both practical and emblematic as it was the sound of the bells for the Catholic service of Matins. The bells rang from the church of Saint Germain l'Auxerrois shortly before dawn broke across the city. As this was a daily call of prayer, both the people of the city and the Huguenots would not have suspected that this was the Catholic signal to attack.

One of the first Huguenots to suffer the wrath of the Catholic troops was Admiral De Coligny – and this time he did not escape death. The admiral's lifeless remains were unceremoniously thrown out of the window of his sick room, which in turn seemed to encourage the Parisian Catholic mob to hunt down more Huguenots. The massacre continued for three long days and nights. Known Huguenots were trapped in their homes and businesses and killed; the few that tried to escape were caught and murdered and their remains were gathered up and dumped in the River Seine. The new royal bridegroom Henri Navarre only managed to escape the slaughter by vowing to convert to the Catholicism, a false promise he never kept.

After the violence and killing had abated, the king held a meeting of the Parisian parliament called *un lit de justice* - literally translated as the bed of justice. During the hearing of the lit de justice, the king issued royal edicts and set down the official recording of the massacre. In these official records, the king claimed he had ordered this bloodshed as he had learnt that the Huguenots were plotting to harm him and the rest of the royal family.

The violence was not isolated to Paris, anti-Protestant violence spread throughout France between the end of August until October of that year, causing similar bloody scenes in Anger, Bordeaux, Bourge, La Charite, Gaillac, Lyon, Meaux, Orleans, Rouen, Toulouse and Troyes. There is no official figure, recording the number of people murdered during the Parisian massacre or those killed within the provinces as the violence spread.

The reason why this French violence was so relevant to the reign of Elizabeth I of England was because it would affect the politics and conviction of one of her closest aids, Francis Walsingham. The horror and fear he must have felt while in Paris, during the massacre as a Protestant, is unimaginable. When the massacre took place Elizabeth, had already been issued with the papal bull from Pope Pius which encouraged her Catholic subjects to rebel and kill her. These events put both Walsingham and Cecil on high alert. It thanks to their doggedly anti-Catholic policies that no less than six Catholic plots to assassinate Queen Elizabeth were uncovered during the rest of her reign.

1584: The Assassination of 'William The Silent'

Even though the Lutheran Reformation happened in 1517, most of mainland continental Europe, particularly in the south, remained predominantly Catholic after the religious struggles that followed the reformation. However, Elizabeth's England was not the only Protestant nation in 1584; Scotland, parts of the Germanic territories and the Netherlands were also Protestant at this time.

William of Orange had inherited the position of Stadtholder of Holland upon the death of Rene of Chalon. Stadtholder was originally a local and somewhat minor authoritative position that dated back to the medieval period, but eventually, the role evolved into becoming the ruler of the United Provinces, which is today known as the Netherlands. As Stadholder, William, who was also known as William The Silent (it is thought because William refused to dignify Spanish and Catholic invaders with a reply when they asked him to persecute the Protestants living within his territories) worked with the Spanish overlords of the territories but became increasingly frustrated by their intolerance towards the Protestant subjects. During the latter part of the 1560s, the Dutch Protestants, which were made up of Protestant Calvinists and Anabaptists, started to deface and destroy religious icons within the churches and cathedrals in an act of protest against the persecution they received from the Catholic Spanish. This act of mass iconoclasm became known as Beeldenstorm. Consequently, religious tensions and unrest within the Dutch territories increased in this period. This was one of the catalysts that started a Protestant revolt for independence in 1568 against the Spanish and the Habsburg dynasty.

In December 1580, William published a letter justifying why he felt he had to take matters into his own hands, effectively he became a rebel leader in doing so. Philip II disliked William for rising up against Spanish rule, and for his Protestantism. On the 15 March 1580, the Spanish King published a proclamation, offering a very generous reward of 25,000 crowns to anyone brave enough to assassinate William of Orange. There was one man who was willing to risk his life and soul to carry out Philip's request, and his name was Balthasar Gerard.

Gerard was a fanatical Catholic who idolised Philip II and his counter-reformation. Over four years, he looked at various different ways in which he could to get close enough to William so that he could to kill him. Two months before the assassination, Gerard presented himself to William, pretending to be a member of the French nobility. His ruse was made all the more authentic, when Gerard presented the Stadtholder with the seal of Count of Mansfelt. Having gained William's trust, the Stadholder entrusted him to deliver a message to his French supporters, who were also against Philip II. William had unintentionally sent his assassin to buy his murder weapon.

Two months passed and Gerard returned to the Netherlands, after carrying out William's request, he was now fully equipped to carry out Philip II's order. During his return visit, Gerard was able to make an appointment to see the Stadtholder in his private residency known as the Prinsenhof; and the fateful appointment was made for 10 July 1584. Gerard waited until William had finished dinning with a guest, an envoy from the Dutch province of Friesland, Rombertus Van Uylenburgh. Van Uylenburgh left the dining room and moments later he heard the two shots fired by Gerard. As the Stadholder died in his home from two close range shots to his torso, Gerard attempted to flee the scene of his crime.

William's last words are record in the official documents of the event as, 'Mon Dieu, ayez pitié de mon âme; mon Dieu, ayez pitié de ce pauvre peuple.' (My God, have pity on my soul; my God, have pity on this poor people). *(Minutes of the States-General of 10 July 1584, quoted in J. W. Berkelbach van der Sprenkel, De Vader des Vaderlands, Haarlem 1941, p. 29).*

Gerard failed to leave Delft and was caught by the authorities and imprisoned. Between being caught and executed, Gerard was tortured by the state. First, he was attached to a pole and lashed, then his hands and feet were bound so that he was unable to sleep. His flesh was branded, and weights were attached to his feet while he hung from the pole. Three days after killing William The Silent, Gerard was put on trial, where he was found guilty of killing William and his was sentence was death. The following day, he was executed in a most brutal fashion. First the executioner, skilled in the art of slow painful deaths, removed Gerard's right hand. Next, chunks of his flesh were forcibly torn from his body before he was disembowelled and had his heart taken out of his chest while he was still, just about alive. After he died, Gerard's remains were then quartered and his head decapitated from his torso. Philip II gave the 27-year-old's parents landed estates in Lievremont, Hostal, and Dampmartin instead of the 25,000 crowns he had initially promised. He also elevated their social status to that of the Spanish nobility.

The assassination of William The Silent was important to Elizabeth's reign as he was a Protestant ruler assassinated as the direct result of a proclamation from a Catholic ruler, in this case, Philip II. At this time, Elizabeth had lived under threat from her papal bull and excommunication for fourteen years. The pope had encouraged her Catholic subjects to kill her. William's murder showed that assassins were a real threat, and that William Cecil, by then known as Lord Burghley, and Sir Francis Walsingham were both doing a very effective job in protecting their queen. The pair had previously foiled several attempts to attack Elizabeth. They knew how to ensure that Elizabeth didn't end up like William the Silent; and for that reason, they needed to eliminate the biggest magnet to Catholic plotters against Elizabeth - Mary, Queen of Scots.

1586: The Babington Plot

The impact of the papal bull and excommunication issued against Elizabeth in 1570 had the effect that the pope wanted, as plots against the English Queen increased, both in Europe and England itself. As well as the Ridolfi Plot of 1571, there was also the Throckmorton Plot which was foiled in 1583, that had followed in a similar vein. The goal was to remove Elizabeth and replace her with Mary with help from the Spanish. Once again, Walshingham's network of skilled spies was able to infiltrate and stop the plot before it could be carried out. But Lord Burghley and Walsingham both knew that as long as Mary Queen of Scots was in England, she would always be able to attract radical Catholics to help her escape from her house-arrest and worse.

The reason that Burghley and Walshingham hadn't managed to charge Mary Queen of Scots was that they never had enough incriminating evidence against her. But they both knew that it was only a matter of time until some other lovesick Catholic youth would try to help Mary again, and next time they intended to lay a trap for her as well as her plotters. In 1586, one such plot came to the attention of Walsingham's spies. Between the spymaster and Burghley they were able to get the incriminating evidence they needed to resolve the problem of what to do with Mary Stuart.

Anthony Babington was a Catholic from Derbyshire who was part of a new generation of men, who had only lived during Protestant Elizabethan rule and had only known Mary Queen of Scots as being a political and religious captive in England. These young men were filled with the optimistic hope that all young people have, as well as a strong religious conviction encouraged by the papal bull. At 24, Anthony Babington had over-romanticised and fallen in love with the mythologised image of Mary, and felt it his was his duty to rescue her from captivity and to help her take the English throne. This impressionable and eager young man had met Mary while he was working within the household the Earl of Shrewsbury and his wife, Bess Hardwick. After leaving the Shrewsbury's employ, Babington became involved with other Catholics both at home in England and over the channel in Europe while acting as a courier for Mary.

Walsingham's spies had made him aware that something was being plotted when his men had detained an English Catholic named Gilbert Gifford as he was re-entering England. Walsingham knew that Gifford was well connected with both European and English Catholic networks and he struck a deal with him. To save his own neck, Gifford became a double agent.

Anthony Babington may have given his name to the plot but there were other men involved in this treason. They were an international collection of radical Catholics including the former Spanish ambassador to England, Bernardino de Mendoza. Mendoza was to assist with the planning from Europe. He had taken part in the failed Throckmorton Plot, and was willing to assist anyone looking to harm Elizabeth I. There was also a Welshman involved by the name of Thomas Morgan. Morgan had become a spy for Mary while she was in captivity. Although he had been caught and had spent three years as a resident within the Tower of London, he had managed to leave the infamous tower, with his head still attached to his body and was exiled to France. Here he met with Babington. Another plotter was Charles Paget. He was another English Catholic who was exiled in France, mainly residing in Paris and the western city of Rouen. He met with Babington, Morgan and Walshingham's double agent, Gifford in Paris to help with the details of their plan to liberate England from Elizabeth's Protestant tyranny. It was not just the Spanish that had a keen interest in removing Elizabeth, another of the co-conspirators was the French ambassador to England at the time, Charles de l'aubespine, Baron de Chateauneuf.

Finally, in the summer of 1586, after months of spying, Walshingham and Gifford's hard work started to produce the results that was needed to entrap the former Scottish queen. The plotters felt it was time to contact Mary, telling her about their support and seeing if she would approve of their plans. By the summer of 1586, Mary was no longer the long-term 'guest' of the Earl of Shrewsbury and his wife, Bess Harwick. Instead she had been moved on to live under the harsher regime of Sir Amyas Paulet - a stern Protestant who kept an especially close eye on his Catholic charge. Under the watch of Paulet, at Chartley House, Mary's correspondence had become near impossible, so Gifford and Walshingham had to find an alternative method to smuggle letters in and out of her new prison. They used a local brewer who supplied Paulet with ale for daily drinking. The coded letters were hidden within the stoppers of the barrels, and one of Mary's household would retire them from the cellar without suspicion or detection. Before each letter met its recipient, the correspondence would be copied by Gifford before carrying on its journey. The encrypted messages were then given to Walshingham's most skilled decoders to translate. The trap was set, and the spymaster just needed to wait for Mary to incriminate herself in writing so that he could arrest and charge her with high treason. It was Chateauneuf who started the correspondence with Mary. This behaviour may be considered entrapment in today's political and judicial law, but Walshingham and Burghley saw it as a means to an end to protect both Elizabeth and the Protestant faith in England.

The incriminating letter was sent from Mary on 28 June to Babington, confirming interest in the plan and asking for more details - Mary had taken the bait. Information about invasion parties, her rescue from Chartley House and Elizabeth's assassination were all sent back to Mary in a coded letter. Her fateful reply was sent back on 17 July when she acknowledged the plans and encouraged the assassination of Elizabeth; Walshingham now had the proof he needed.

> 'I would be glad to know the names and quelityes of the six gentlemen which are to accomplish the dessignement, for that it maybe, i shall be able uppon knowledge of the parties to give you some further advise necessarye to be followed therein; and even so do I wish to be made acquainted with the names of all such principle persons.' *(Pollen J Hungerford (1922) Publication of the Scottish Historical Society third series vol III: Mary Queen of Scots & the Babington Plot T&A constable Ltd PP45-6)*

Arrests followed and Mary was still unaware that the conspiracy had been discovered and that she was a wanted woman. On 11 August 1586, she had been allowed to go out riding. Not realising that her co-conspirators had been arrested and charged, Mary was expecting a rescue party to arrive and save her. When she saw riders on the horizon, she must have thought they were there to set her free. Unfortunately, they were in fact Elizabeth's men, there to arrest her. There was much discussion as to what to do with Mary. This can be seen in the following quotation taken from the Domestic State Papers in a letter dated Sept 9, from Windsor 'Burghley to Walshingham - Long discussion with the Queen touching the bringing of the Queen of Scots to some apt place where her cause and herself might be heard. Many places named but none agreed on.' *(Calendar of State papers domestic series Elizabeth 1581-90)*. Eventually, all parties decided to relocate the fallen Queen of Scots to Fotheringay Castle.

On the day before he was executed, Anthony Babington wrote to Queen Elizabeth from the Tower of London, begging for mercy and imploring her to forgive him on behalf of his poor wife and his innocent children. *(Calendar of State papers domestic series Elizabeth 1581-90)* The following day, Babington was taken from The Tower and brought to St Giles Fields near Holborn to be executed, suffering the fate of all common traitors, by being hung, drawn before death, disembowelled and castrated before being beheaded. His body was then quartered, and the parts and his head were tarred so that they could be displayed as a warning to others. He was only 25.

It was at Fotheringay, that Mary would face trial for her treasonous involvement in the plot. Three days after Babington's execution, the following correspondence was sent '23 Sept Thomas Wylkes to Edward Norrey Esq. A commission of Lords of Council and other noblemen to meet at Fotheringhay Castle to proceed to the Queen of Scots. A new Parliament summoned for 15 October to confirm attainder.'

The trial was held in October and Elizabeth was represented at the trial, which took place in the great hall of the castle, by Burghley and Walsingham. The other commissioners appointed by Elizabeth to oversee the trial of Mary and to ensure that the trial was both fair and lawful were: the Archbishop of Canterbury, Sir Thomas Bromley, William, Lord Marquis of Winchester, Edward, Earl of Oxford, George, Earl of Shrewsbury, Henry, Earl of Kent, William, Earl of Worcester, Edward, Earl of Rutland, Ambrose, Earl of Warwick, Henry, Earl of Pembrook, Robert, Earl of Leicester, Henry, Earl of Lincoln, Anthony, Viscount Montague, Charles, Lord Howard, Henry, Lord Hudson, Henry, Lord Abergavenny, Edward, Lord Zouch, Edward, Lord Morley, William,

Lord Cobham, Edward, Lord Stafford, Arthur, Lord Grey of Wilton, John, Lord Lumley, John, Lord Sturton, William, Lord Sandes, Henry, Lord Wentford, Lewis, Lord Mordant, Thomas, Lord Buckhurst, Henry, Lord Compton, Henry, Lord Chesney, Sir Francis Knolles, Sir James Crofts, Sir Christopher Hatton, William Davison Esq, Sir Ralph Sadler, Sir Walter Mildmay, Sir Amyas Paulet, John Wolley, Sir Christopher Wray, Sir Edmund Anderson, Sir Roger Manwood, Sir Thomas Gawdy and Justice William Periam.

Mary represented herself at her trial and she gave one of the best performances of her life. On the first day of the trial on 11 October she addressed the gathered commissioners saying: 'It grieveth me that the Queen, my most dear sister, is misinformed of me and that I have been so many years kept in prison.' *(State trials of Mary Queen of Scots, Sir Walter Raleigh an Captain William Kidd. Francis Hargrave esq, London 1776)* she went on to say 'As for this letter, it seemth strange to me that the queen should command me as a subject to appear personally in judgement. I am an absolute Queen and will do nothing which may prejudice either mine own royal majesty or other Princes of my place and rank or my son.' *(State trials of Mary Queen of Scots, Sir Walter Raleigh and Captain William Kidd. Francis Hargrave esq, London 1776)*

Mary's next line of defence was 'The laws and statutes of England are to me most unknown; I am destitute of councillors.' *(State trials of Mary Queen of Scots, Sir Walter Raleigh and Captain William Kidd. Francis Hargrave esq, London 1776)* She finishes addressing the commissioners by reinforcing that as a queen she cannot be tried by men of lesser status than herself even with written evidence. 'I am not to be charged but by my own word or writing which can not be produced against me. Yet I can not deny but I have commended myself and my cause to foreign Princes.' *(State trials of Mary Queen of Scots, Sir Walter Raleigh an Captain William Kidd. Francis Hargrave esq, London 1776)*

On the following day, 12 October, the commissioners addressed several of the points that Mary had raised the day before by saying, 'But the Lord Chancellor and Treasurer declare their authority by patent, and showed that neither imprisonment nor her prerogative of Royal Majesty could exempt her from answering in this kingdom; with fair words advising her to hear what matters were to be objected against her.' *(State trials of Mary Queen of Scots, Sir Walter Raleigh and Captain William Kidd. Francis Hargrave esq, London 1776)* Mary's answer to this was simple and set the tone for how she behaved for the rest of her life. 'She answered that she was no subject and rather she die a thousand deaths, than acknowledge herself a subject considering that by such an acknowledgement she should both prejudice the height of regal majesty and withal confess herself to be bound by all the laws of England even in the matter of religion: nevertheless she was ready to answer all things in a free and full parliament.' *(State trials of Mary Queen of Scots, Sir Walter Raleigh an Captain William Kidd. Francis Hargrave esq, London 1776)* Mary went on over the course of her trial, bravely defending herself as a queen, and claiming to be innocent of the crimes she had been charged with.

Despite her best efforts to argue her case, Mary was still found guilty of high treason on 25 October. This left Elizabeth in an uncomfortable position - she now had to sign a death warrant for a fellow God-anointed queen, and a on a more personal note, she would be authorising the death of her own cousin. Elizabeth had already struggled with the pressure and personal emotions involved when she'd signed the Duke of Norfolk's death warrant in 1572. Mary's death warrant was complicated further because Elizabeth would be virtually starting a religious war with the rest of Catholic Europe with her signature; a war that Elizabeth was ill-prepared for both militarily and financially. The situation must have reminded Elizabeth of her step-sister's actions towards Lady Jane Grey. Elizabeth was no fool, she had now survived three plots to kill her, all involving her cousin Mary replacing her on the throne; by keeping her alive, Elizabeth knew she was increasing the risk to her person and to the future of the Protestant faith in England. She knew that there would be more impressionable young men willing to try and help the Queen of Scots, justifying their actions as an act of faith as such actions were sanctified by the papal bull. Keeping Mary alive and captive had now become too dangerous. Both Walsingham and Burghley reasoned with Elizabeth and there was only so much the queen could do to avoid her responsibility, and not see justice carried out. She eventually signed the death warrant in February 1587, and Walshingham and Burghley wasted no time in making the execution happen at Fotheringay Castle on 8 February 1587.

1587: The Execution of Mary Queen of Scots

Mary, Queen of Scots was executed at Fortheringhay Castle. She faced her death with so much passion, show, class and bravery that her incredible dignity is remembered to this day. After being found guilty of high treason in the autumn of 1586, the sentence of death hung over Mary for several months as Elizabeth struggled to actually sign her death warrant. Elizabeth signed and destroyed two warrants, stating that she was unable to follow through on the execution on the grounds that Mary was a queen and that God alone should end her life.

Evidence of this struggle can be found in a letter Elizabeth wrote in January 1587 to the French king and Mary's former brother-in-law, Henri III: 'It is impossible to save my own life if I preserve that of the Queen of Scots, but if you ambassadors can point out any means whereby I may do it consistently with my own security, I shall be greatly obliged to you never having shed so many tears at the death of my father, my brother King Edward or my sister Mary as I have done for this unfortunate affair' *(Strickland A, Live of the Queens of England, 1866, P471)*

Finally, on 4 February 1587, Elizabeth once again signed the warrant and Burghley was able to retrieve the document before Elizabeth had time to destroy it. He had the warrant dispatched by Robert Beale who was ordered to first take it to the Earls of Shrewsbury and Kent before going onto Fotheringhay Castle. When the men arrived at Fotheringhay they went directly to the Scottish queen's goaler, Amyst Paulet, before going to inform Mary she was soon to die. After listening to the reading of the warrant, Mary is said to have asked whether she was to meet the same fate as Richard II, who had been murdered in Pontefract Castle. After being reassured that this was not what Elizabeth or the English privy council intended for her, she calmly said 'I thank you for such welcome news. You will do me a great good in withdrawing me from this world, out of which I am very glad to go.' *(BL MS 48027/FOS 639)*

The months of not knowing her fate seem to have prepared Mary for this moment; if this was going to be her ending, then Mary was going to leave this world with true dignity and style. She had after all been brought up within the French court and was more French than Scottish in many ways. In her final hours she had a purpose, she knew what she had to do. 'I am quite ready and very happy to die, and to shed my blood for Almighty God, my Saviour and my Creator, and for the Catholic Church and to maintain its rights in this country.' *(BL MS 48027/FOS 639)*

Firstly, she asked for her chaplain to see her and to offer her comfort. This request was callously denied by her Protestant gaoler Sir Amyas Paulet. She had also asked to be buried with either her first husband Francis or her mother, both of whom were buried in France. Shrewsbury informed her that she was being unreasonable to expect Elizabeth to send her executed body to France in order to be buried.

When the men finally left her chambers, Mary refused to weep with her gentlewomen. She spent a couple of hours in prayer and ate very little. Her prayers comforted and helped her plan her final hours. The first thing she needed to do was to write her last will and testament. Then she went through her wardrobe and her last few processions and distributed them amongst her loyal servants. One of the last letters she wrote was to her former brother-in-law, the King of France, Henri III. The saddest lines of this tear-stained letter were in reference to her son, James. They read: 'Concerning my son, I commend him to you inasmuch as he deserves it, as I cannot answer for him.' *(NLS MS 54.1.1)*

Practically she had prepared as best as she could, and now, all she could do was wait. She lay on her bed very still and dozed until 6.00 am when she got up to be helped by her serving women for the very last time. On first appearances, she looked like she was dressed all in black except for a while veil that went down her back to the floor and was held in place with a small white cap. Her gown was of thick black satin, trimmed with gold embroidery and sable. Her outer bodice was crimson, and her sleeves were Italian in style, slashed and revealing glimpses of purple velvet. Her shoes for this final walk were of Spanish suede and her stockings were the colour of sky blue, embroidered with silver thread and kept up with green garters. But she still had a secret close to her skin not to be revealed until moments before she met her maker. Her make-up and wig were made to complete the look, and to try and turn back the effects of so many years in prison. She may have been 44-years-old but the last eighteen years of captivity had taken their toll on Mary's appearance and she looked considerably older.

Once dressed Mary gathered her small household together and bid them farewell before having her will read for them all to hear and witness. Then they all knelt in prayer. They had only just started when there was a knock at her chamber's door. Upon leaving her quarters, Mary prepared herself to project the ideal image of a Catholic martyr. She carried with her an ivory crucifix and a Latin book of prayers. At her waist, she wore a rosary adorned with a gold cross. While making her way to her place of execution, Mary met James Melville, (a diplomat from Scotland who had served Mary over the years since her return from France) who was weeping. Mary is said to have said the following to the distraught man: 'You ought to rejoice rather than weep for that the end of Mary Stuart's troubles is now come... tell my friends that I die a true woman to my religion and like a true Scottish woman and a true French woman." *(Camden W, History of Most Renowned and Vicious Princess Elizabeth, 1675 p285)*

She entered the hall with two of her gentlewomen and Melville holding her train. She mounted the black velvet draped platform that had been erected for the purpose of her death. The warrant was read then the prayers were supposed to have started. The minister who was chosen for this grim task was Dr Richard Fletcher, Dean of Peterborough and a favourite of Elizabeth. He stumbled over the opening of his prayers and Mary quickly put him in his place by saying: 'Mr Dean, I will not hear you. You have nothing to do with me, nor I with you... I am settled in the ancient Roman Catholic religion and mind to spend my blood in defence of it.' *(Dunn J Elizabeth & Mary P496)*. The dean was said to have asked her to reject her faith and die in the Protestant faith of the Queen of England. Understandably, Mary coloured with anger and he was encouraged by the Earls of Shrewsbury and Kent get on with the prayers.

As the prayers started, the dean started in English, while Mary loudly began her final prayers in Latin, clutching her crucifix before her face. The witnesses in the hall responded to the dean's prayers in English while Mary and her servants continued their prayers in Latin. She is said to have slipped to her knees and continued after the dean had finished.

Her final insult to the dean was after she had finished praying when she pronounced that she hoped there would be an end to the religious unrest in England, for her son James to find the Catholic faith, that Elizabeth continue to reign before finally asking for the saints to pray for her soul before kissing her crucifix and making the sign of the cross in the Catholic fashion. Mary now turned to her executioner who was begging her forgiveness to whom she said: 'I forgive you with all my heart for now, I hope, you shall make an end of all my troubles.'" *(R Wynkfielde MS 81 Account of the Trial, Execution and Burial of MQS)*

Now Mary performed her last act, which was the ultimate insult to this Protestant audience; Mary's gentle women undressed her to reveal a scarlet petticoat - red being the colour of Catholic martyrs. We only know this from the accounts of her French servants as the Protestant recorders were told to omit it from the official report.

The moment that both Burghley and Walshingham had wanted for so long was nigh. Mary thanked and blessed her servants before she went to kneel on the cushion by the block. Her eyes were covered with the white Corpus Christi cloth. After reciting Psalm *In te Domino confido In Thee, O Lord, have I put my trust*, she laid down her head on the block; stretched out her arms and legs before saying *In manus tutas, Domine commendo spititum meum – Into your hands O Lord I commend my spirit. (R Wynkfielde MS 81 Account of the Trial, Execution and Burial of MQS)*

The axe was raised but poor Mary's ordeal was not over, for the executioner missed her neck causing the axe to hack into the back of her head. The second strike hit the target but did not completely remove her head. This meant that the executioner had to use the axe as a cleaver to complete his gristly task. This was hardly a dignified end for a God-anointed queen.

As the executioner held up her head and proclaimed God save Queen Elizabeth, but he lost his grip as Mary had been wearing an auburn wig. While she had been imprisoned, her red hair had turned prematurely white and she had wanted to hide this right up to her death. Mary was not alone in her final moments her small pet dog named Geddon had been with her in her petticoats, when the executioner moved her corpse, he found the poor creature covered in his mistresses' blood. The dog was taken away and washed but died within days of Mary.

All the items that Mary had with her at her death, including her crucifix and Latin prayer book as well as the executioner's block and

Mary's blood-stained clothes were removed from the scaffold in the great hall and taken outside and burnt. This was so that they could not become Catholic relics. Her body was then moved for it to be embalmed.

On the 10 February, Elizabeth learnt that Mary had died, and she was angry with Burghley and her privy council who had acted upon the signed death warrant without her consent. Burghley and the council had done this so that they could be blamed for Mary's death rather than the queen. Elizabeth is said to have refused to speak to Burghley for days after Mary's execution and William Davison, her personal secretary, was even sent to the Tower of London for his part in the act.

Elizabeth's emotions over the next few days must have been very strong; it is hard to imagine what she felt. Her feelings must have swayed between guilt, anger, relief, frustration, sadness and grief. Some of these feelings are expressed in a letter written to Mary's son James on 14 February 1587: 'My Dear Brother, I would you know (though not felt) the extreme dolour that overwhelms my mind for that miserable accident which (far contrary to my meaning) hath befallen...I beseech you that as God and many more know, how innocent I am in this case: so you will believe me, that if I had bid aught I would have bid by it.' *(Harrison GB ed., The Letters of Queen Elizabeth 1935 p188)*

Mary's first resting place was in Peterborough Cathedral where she remained until the end of Elizabeth's reign. It was her son, James I, who had her remains exhumed and moved to be buried at Westminster Abbey meters away from Elizabeth's final resting place - the two queens were closer in death than they had been in life.

The consequences of Mary's execution would affect the last sixteen years of Elizabeth's reign. The biggest of these consequences happened the following year when Philip II of Spain used Mary's death as an excuse to launch an armada against the English off the south coast. He hoped to invade England and depose Elizabeth from the throne, and thus placing England under Spanish rule.

1588: The Spanish Armada

After decades of cold war animosity, the political and more importantly, the religious differences between Elizabethan England and Catholic Spain almost came close to full-blown war, when Philip II raised a Catholic naval invasion force, the Spanish Armada, to invade England on a religious crusade. He wanted to save the souls of Protestant England while expanding his global empire. It was the summer of 1688, and the Spanish Armada was the most powerful naval fleet of the age.

While Philip II was at the peak of his success in 1588, Elizabeth's treasury was empty. She had no professional standing army and she feared that her Catholic subjects would utilise this opportunity to return England to Rome. This was also a matter of life and death, as defeat at the hands of the Spanish would also have been the end of Elizabeth's reign with at best imprisonment awaiting her and more probably death. It would also mark the end of the Tudor dynasty. It was hardly going to be a fair battle and England, was at this point, the Protestant underdog of the two sides. The crisis that would unfold, became one of the defining events of Elizabeth's long reign as well as part of English historic folklore.

On Friday 29 July 1588, Elizabeth's court was located at Richmond Palace, just west of London upon the banks of the River Thames. This was where the now 54-year-old monarch felt most happy and was somewhere she often went when she needed to feel safe. She kept her most trusted ladies around her, including her confident, and highest-ranking lady-in-waiting, Blanche Perry.

Elizabeth was in Richmond when Philip's crusading armada left Spain. It was comprised of 125 ships and 23,000 well-trained men and enough arms, money and supplies to enable an invasion with a further army ready for attack. This additional force was waiting in the Spanish territories of the Netherlands. While this elite naval power was sailing towards the English south coast, the English navy was in poor shape.

News of the invasion had been rumoured throughout the summer of 1588. The English had tried to intercept the Spanish at sea and had attempted to keep them away from the English coastline. Unfortunately, they had not seen one Spanish ship heading towards England; that was soon to change. To add to the bad luck the English were having, poor weather had damaged the small English fleet as it was waiting for sight of the Spanish vessels, so by end of July 1588, the naval ships docked in Plymouth were far from battle ready.

The commander of the Royal Navy at this time was Charles Howard, Lord Howard of Effingham who also happened to be Queen Elizabeth's cousin. This was a strange position for him to hold as he had no naval experience. Thankfully, his second in command, Sir Francis Drake made up for Howard's lack of experience as he was England's best privateer; and was little better than a state-approved pirate. As a loyal Protestant who had frequently come into conflict with the Spanish at sea, he also had a grudge against Spain, making him the perfect man for the job. The English did have a further smaller fleet of thirty-five ships. This fleet was docked just off the Kent coast to be used to defend the mouth of the River Thames and protect the water access to London. On the 29 July, the rest of the English naval fleet were moored in Plymouth Harbour, being repaired, while the mighty Spanish Armanda was only forty miles away and getting closer by the hour.

The commander of the Spanish Armanda was the Duke of Medina Sidona. He too had no naval experience and had got his post due to his noble birth, just like Howard. The duke was not a natural sailor. He had written a pleading missive to Philip II asking to be relieved of his duty as the commander of the armada. Like Howard, Medina Sidona had a highly experienced sailor for his second in command - Juan Martenez de Recalde. Recalde's experience led him to suggest that the Spanish should attack the English while they were within the harbour at Plymouth and (unbeknown to the Spanish) ill-prepared at this time. However, this attack never came about due to the Duke of Medina Sidona as he refused to venture away from the plans for the mission laid out by Philip II. This was the first of several missed opportunities during the attempted invasion and Recalde would become increasing resentful at having the inexperienced duke overrule his sensible tactics during the twelve-day crisis.

There was a second part to the Spanish plan of invasion. Philip had planned for a two-force attack on heretical England using both naval and armed forces to crush Elizabeth. He had troops waiting in the Spanish territories within the Netherlands. The idea was to aim for Margate in the English county of Kent and to advance towards London and Elizabeth. Philip also hoped that the suppressed English Catholics would join their fellow Catholic invaders in bringing down Elizabeth the Protestant queen. So, the job of the English navy during the crisis was to keep the Spanish navy from joining up with these armed men and landing on English soil; as once on terra firma, it was unlikely that the English could have successfully defeated the military might of Spain.

During the 29 July, bad weather caused the English fleet to stay within Plymouth's harbour when the Spanish fleet was spotted that evening. When both Elizabeth and Philip retired for the evening, they were no closer to knowing how they stood after the first day of the crisis.

As the 30 July broke over the south coast of England, the armada continued its mission towards the English Channel and onto Margate. Although it had been spotted by the enemy, the Spanish had not yet seen an English ship. The English were by this point as prepared as they could be, and the fleet finally left the safety and shelter of Plymouth and was heading straight towards the Spanish invasion party. The royal navy, as the weaker side, had no intention of going face to face with its stronger enemy.

The first strategy of the English plan was to stop the Spanish from taking over any of its coastal harbours deep enough to dock a great fleet of ships and subsequently using this as a military base. The best way to do this was by not being reduced in numbers through battle but by getting behind the enemy and chasing its ships away from the ports. It was unfortunate that the English didn't realise that capturing an English port was not on the Spanish agenda. As the second day wore on, the English ships had caught up with the armada at 15:00, just as the weather started to take a nasty turn for the worse. It was at this moment that the English decided to begin their chasing tactic from behind. The ships on both sides had between twenty and fifty cannons per ship and they had the ability to fire iron cannonballs of up to 60lbs in weight. Although the armada was impressive in experience and in its size, it was the English who had more modern weaponry, in particular, specifically made ship cannons. The English cannons were made by casting molten iron rather than the traditional method of hand beating the body of the guns. The English had designed and made cannon that had been adapted for ease of use on their new ships unlike the Spanish guns that were bulky, had wheels and were cumbersome to use and reload quickly during battle.

News had now reached the Richmond Palace, that the Spanish had been spotted. Before this update was passed onto the Elizabeth, it would have been trusted to the two most powerful men in the queen's court, Lord Burghley, her Lord Treasurer, and Sir Francis Walshingham her Secretary of State and Spymaster General. Burghley in his office of Lord Treasurer knew just how little money there was in the national vault. He, like Elizabeth, was eager to ensure that this crisis cost the crown as little as possible. Walshingham, was Burghley's opposite, he knew in order for the English to defeat Spain's military might, Elizabeth needed to authorise money to be spent on essentials such as arms, ammunition and sailors, in order to prevent this attack from turning into a protracted war, that would see both Protestant England and Elizabeth in ruin. Walshingham had witnessed first-hand how fanatical Catholics treated Protestants as he had been in Paris during the bloody St Bartholomew's Day massacre and seen 'les rues du Paris' run red with Protestant Huguenot blood. As day two of the crisis came to a close, little had changed apart from the fact that the Spanish were closer, and Elizabeth was understandably afraid of what may happen in the coming hours and days.

Day three was Sunday 31 July and, the Spanish had sighted the English, who had in turn successfully out foxed them, as they were not where the Spanish had expected to find them. The royal navy located itself behind its Catholic enemy. The Spanish had taken this move as an attack and had started to move into its traditional battle formation - a crescent, spread out over an area approximately two nautical miles in width. It was the English who opened the first battle by firing a single shot towards the armada at 09:00. The shot was fired from a small ship named the Disdain, which, after firing the challenging shot retreated back to the rest of the royal fleet. Traditionally, sea battles between two sides would meet head on and the ships would get as close as possible to allow the sailors to invade the other side's ships. This would then create vicious hand-to-hand fighting on the ships' decks. In this case, the English had no intention of getting that close to the Spanish, they knew they were the underdogs in this fight and needed to use their weapons in the most effective way.

This new tactic deployed by the English worked in a similar way to a moving conveyer belt of ships firing cannon at the Spanish Armada then moving away so the ship behind could next take a shot. There was an unpredictable element to this tactic as the English had never done this before, and they did not know how close they needed to get to the enemy to be able to hit them from a safe distance. The battle continued for several hours, and the soldiers on the Spanish fleet could do nothing but watch as the English kept them from getting too close. It is estimated that the English managed to fire approximately two thousand cannonballs during this first skirmish, whereas the Spanish only managed to fire about seven hundred and fifty rounds in return fire. Despite the length of the first battle neither side had lost a ship in the encounter and the English side had used a lot of its limited ammunition.

Luck would change for the English when later that afternoon, a Spanish ship named San Salvador blew up, although it was unclear what had caused this. A little while later, a second Spanish ship, named The Rosario, crashed, causing great damage to the stability of the vessel. The Spanish reluctantly had to leave the broken ships and continued their journey towards the English Channel. That evening, Howard wrote to court asking for more gunpowder and cannonballs. Drake was a man who lived by his wits and he had an alternative plan to elevate the chronic lack of supplies temporarily; he intended to use his privateering skills to plunder the stricken ship, The Rosario. In doing so, Drake found gunpowder and ammunition as well as vital intelligence that would help the English understand how the Spanish ships were laid out, information that could be used to their advantage. He was also able to plunder 50,000 golden ducats a great wealth of gold for a warship to be carrying.

On the morning of the fourth day of the crisis, Monday 1 August, the English found themselves delayed primarily due to Drake's night time raid. They needed to catch up with the Spanish to keep the pressure on them and stop them from attempting to dock in the naturally deep harbours along the English south coast. They were particularly worried about Weymouth and Portland Bill as well as the possibility of the Spanish potentially capturing the Isle of Wight. If the Spanish took control of the Solent, the English commanders thought an invasion would be easy.

Despite the distance between the two sides, the English were able to catch up with their Catholic nemesis. This was due to the English ships' new design. Their ships were lower in the water, lighter in weight and narrower, than the bulky old style of Spanish galleons; as a result, Howard and Drake were also aided by what has become known as the 'good Protestant wind' that blew them in the right direction.

The English may have been having a bit of luck but the same could not be said of the Spanish. Tensions had increased between the Spanish naval leaders and the disagreements were over how to proceed. Philip II's masterplan included a Spanish army of 27,000 men waiting for the armada in the Spanish territories in the Netherlands. This army was under the command of the Duke of Parma. On paper, having the army and naval powers meet and proceed to invade England looked like it was a foolproof plan, but in reality, things were very different. Communication was slow and neither the Spanish navy nor the Duke of Parma could communicate fast enough or accurately enough to put these plans effectively in place.

Tuesday, 2 August was the fifth day of the crisis in English waters, the two naval powers found themselves off the tip of Portland Bill very close to the deep harbour at Weymouth. The English who believed that this was where the Spanish were headed decided to set a trap to distract the enemy. They did this by sending a small flotilla of ships to Portland Bill. The hope was that this tactic would be enough bait to lure the Spanish away from Weymouth. This diversion was led by Martin Frobisher, an experienced sailor who knew this part of the southern coast extremely well. Frobisher was familiar with the tidal patterns, known locally as the Portland race. He knew that he could use this tide to potentially wreck or at the very least trap any Spanish vessels coming to attack their bait made up of a little flotilla of English ships.

The plan worked, as that is exactly what happened to four Spanish ships; what the English lacked in manpower and arms, they made up for in knowledge of their home waters. While some of the Spanish attempted to reach Frobisher, Drake led a simulations attack on the other side of the armada's fleet. A third prong of attack came from Howard, who surged at the Spanish head on; the Spanish were sitting targets being attacked by gunpowder and ammunition plundered by Drake, from The Rosario. The Spanish could not compete with the speed and ease of the English cannon. The biggest damage that the Battle of Portland Bill caused was malcontent amongst the Spanish, who were beginning to doubt the leadership skills of the Duke of Medina Sidonia, who was still doggedly following the plan prepared by Phillip II.

The plundered ammunition and gunpowder Drake had taken from The Rosario was almost depleted after the Battle of Portland Bill, so Howard urgently sent another letter to court asking for more supplies. Now the English believed that Weymouth was safe, they feared that the Spanish would capture the Isle of Wight and use it as a base to attack the south coast of England. Elizabeth had sent three thousand men to defend the small island from the Spanish, but the island only had four cannons and enough ammunition for one day of combat.

Despite the battles that had been fought so far, very little damage had been done to the crusading Spanish navy. This was especially frustrating considering the amount of ammunition the English had fired. The only way that this could be improved was by knowing how close they needed to get to ensure a more accurate aim at the Armada's ships while remaining at a safe distance. Drake's answer was to use the wrecked San Salvador to calculate the ideal firing distance. During this experimentation, Drake discovered that a distance of 100 feet would provide a more effective aim at the high moving hulls of the Spanish galleys.

By day seven, Wednesday 4 August, the Spanish Armada still had no news from the Duke of Parma and the land contingency of their mission. Even the rigid Duke of Medina Sidonia was becoming frustrated with Philip's plan after following it for six days and achieving very little. In a bold and daring change of plan, Medina Sidonia decided to drop anchor off the Isle of Wight. This was a massive risk, as the Spanish had very little knowledge of these waters and seemed to be unaware of just how dangerous and shallow, the waters were.

The English now had the upper hand, they used the information gathered from Drake's experiments and their knowledge of the local waters to plan how they would attack the armada off the Isle of Wight. They started to hit the ships at the heart of the Spanish fleet. The English attacked the Spanish from multiple directions, taking bigger and bigger risks as they grew desperately short of ammunition. It was then that the weather came to aid the Protestant English by blowing the Catholic fleet into even shallower waters at the eastern end of Isle of Wight. The water was so shallow here that it would only come waist high on an average man, which was bad news for the deep hulled Spanish galleons. The Spanish had no option but to retreat away from the Isle of Wight. The jubilant inhabitants of the island rang their church bells in celebration of the retreating Spaniards.

The Duke of Medina Sidonia took this as a sign from God, that he had to keep following Philip II's original plan, without further question, if they were to succeed in this holy crusade. The next logical plan for the Spanish was to sail to the French port of Calais, so that the fleet could finally communicate and meet up with Duke of Parma and the additional men. Parma would be only twenty-one miles north of the French harbour town. Little happened on the eighth day of the threat. It was Friday 5th August and the Spanish followed by the English moved towards friendly Catholic waters off the north coast of France. The irony was that Calais was once an English territory in France.

Elizabeth had until this point been curmudgeonly with regards to sending her fleet much needed supplies at both Howard and Drake's request. The queen's solution was to send them musketeers instead of gunpowder and cannonballs, proving how little she and her privy council knew of naval planning or warfare.

Day nine of the conflict, Saturday 6 August, was another quiet day as each side took stock of what had passed during the last week of engagement. After dropping anchor off Calais, local dignitaries from the French town sent the Duke of Medina Sidonia messages of welcome. Meanwhile Howard and Drake knew they needed to take risks and act decisively if they were to stop the Spanish Armada and the troops of the Duke of Parma from joining up. Despite three battles, neither side has achieved their aims. Neither side had been critically damaged by the other and at this point there was still a very real risk aimed at the English and Elizabeth.

As day ten dawned on Sunday 7 August, the Spanish should have been within grasping distance of joining up with their land army and the Duke of Parma. However, this part of Philip's plan proved to be unrealistic. This was unbeknown to Howard and Drake, who had been preparing for the worst.

Desperately short of ammunition, it must have felt like a losing battle. Elizabeth was still residing at Richmond Palace. She was now aware that the Spanish were anchored off Calais and she knew of the threat this posed to her country and her personal safety. This news finally made Elizabeth decide to relocate from her favourite palace at Richmond to St James' Palace in the heart of London. St James' was better defended should the worst happen, and the Spanish landed on English soil. Relocating an Elizabethan court was no easy task. There was a lot of logistical and practical planning involved. Personal items for the queen needed to be organised and packed. Then there was the matter of relocating around two hundred attendants and members of her household along with all their personal effects. Court officials needed to notifying St James' Palace so it could be prepared and fortified for the queen and lastly, there was the risky task of moving Elizabeth as safely as they could at this time of crisis. The chosen method of transport was to be by royal barge, travelling easterly along the River Thames. If the queen was safe so was Protestantism in England.

Realistically and with the luxury of hindsight, things were not as dire as the English believed. The two leaders of the Spanish Armada, Medina Sidonia and Recalde, were still at loggerheads over the best course of action to take. There were still communication difficulties between the Spanish fleet and Parma. They had no plan for how they were to meet up and join forces. News had arrived from Parma later that day and it was not good. The 27,000 strong army that the Spanish Armada was supposed to meet, was not ready, and would not be for another week. Nothing had been prepared, mainly because of the lack of communication between the naval fleet and the ground forces, with the army leaders deciding that it was too risky to keep military men loitering indefinitely at a port where they were vulnerable to drunkenness, desertion and brawling. This meant that the armada would have to wait at Calais, sitting like ducks for a whole week and exposed to the English navy from the seaboard side. In short, the Spanish were now very vulnerable.

The strategy that Howard and Drake devised was simple yet known to be very effective. They needed to cause panic deep within the anchored Spanish fleet and then attack while the enemy was still in disarray. They were going to send eight fire ships into the moored armada and then strike the next day. It was a risky move as well as a dangerous one, but they needed to hit the enemy hard and fast in order to be effective against the most powerful navy of the sixteenth century. This was a tactic that had been used since ancient times, most effectively by the ancient Greeks. That evening, both the winds and tides were working in English favour. The eight fire ships were stripped of all their valuable items; their masts, ropes and rigging were covered in highly flammable tar and the bowels of the vessels were filled with flammable materials. A small crew would remain on board as the ships combusted to direct the burning boats into the direction of the anchored enemy ships. The last thing to do was for the remaining men to evacuate the ships via small boats. There was a risk, but it was relatively small. In order to cause the maximum panic, the eight English fire ships were deployed at midnight.

There was a call of alarm amongst the Spanish as day eleven dawned. It was minutes into Monday 8 August when the Spanish had spotted the fire ships. They were able to eliminate two of the eight burning boats before they reached the anchored vessels but the remaining six did exactly what the English had hoped; they caused maximum fear and confusion. In their panic, many of the armada's ships cut their anchor ropes rather than bring them up. This effectively meant that they were now unable to re-anchor or effectively stop. Part one of the English tactic had worked; the Spanish were scattered and vulnerable and the English, were for the first time in this crisis, strong enough to launch a full-on attack at the crusading invaders.

The Spanish fleet was now scattered. Only five ships were left moored within Calais harbour. Amongst those five vessels was the flagship of the fleet, captained by the Duke of Medina Sidonia. These remaining ships now faced the whole of Elizabeth's naval power. The fight became known as the Battle of Gravelines. This battle was the climax of thirty years of personal, political and religious grudges between the Queen of England and the Spanish King.

Howard and Drake were now aided by an additional thirty-five ships from Kent, which brought much needed supplies of ammunition, food and fresh drinking water. The battle started at 06.00, only six hours after the English had reaped mayhem with their fire ships. Using what they had learnt from the previous three battles, Drake started off hard and fast, firing at the five ships while the rest of the navy attacked them from all sides. The English cannon were able to fire off five times faster than the Spaniards.

The rest of the scattered Spanish Armada had started to re-group and form a battle position to counter-attack the English, but the weather and tides were once again working against them. They were further hampered by the closeness of the battle as the constant use of cannon produced a lot of dense smoke making it hard to see clearly. The skies were dark due to an oncoming rainstorm and both sides were battered with fierce winds. The battle continued until 05.00.

While her navy was winning the Battle of Gravelines, Elizabeth traveled to St James' with her retinue. She knew nothing of the killer blow that her navy had struck against the Spanish. The queen must have been feeling extremely vulnerable and worried, not just for her safety but for the souls of her Protestant nation. Fearing that the worst was about to happen, Walsingham and Burghley prepared anti-Spanish propaganda to be printed and distributed throughout London and the rest of the kingdom. Their hope was that even Catholics, sympathetic to Philip's crusade would be prepared to fight for the English against *child-killing* Spaniards. Later that day Elizabeth was informed of the English victory at Gravelines but with caution, as despite this great victory, the Spanish could still regroup and attempt to re-invade England. The damaged armada was heading north up the east coast of England toward Scotland. Elizabeth, who was naturally thrifty and dreaded getting into more debt, now refused to supply anymore necessities to her navy, the navy who had just saved her country and her life. This was a big gamble. Thankfully for Elizabeth, the weather intervened - if the Spanish had been intending on regrouping and trying to invade again, the northerly 'Protestant' wind had other ideas. A council of war amongst the Spanish commanders took place and Medina Sidonia decided that his duty now was to reluctantly admit defeat and return as many of the remaining ships back to Spain.

By the time that the defeated Spanish fleet reached Newcastle on the north east coast of England, they needed to throw heavy items such as weapons and even their horses overboard as they were running low on supplies of food and water. They hoped that by making the ships lighter they would get home faster. Their safest route home was up around Scotland and down and around the rocky and dangerous coastline of Northern Ireland towards the Irish county of Mayo.

One of the best known Spanish wrecks off the coast of Mayo was of the El Gran Grin, a 1200 tonne Spanish behemoth. In all, twenty ships were lost off the tempestuous Irish west coastline and it is estimated that fifteen hundred Spanish men drowned. Those who survived a shipwreck were not any luckier than their drowned shipmates. Men of status were ransomed by the Irish for high stakes, while regular sailors were either murdered by the Irish or executed by the Protestant English soldiers, stationed in Ireland. Five months after they had set out to conquer heathen England, the battered and humiliated armada limped back to Spain with only sixty-three ships. They had lost 20,000 men in their failed crusade against Elizabeth.

Elizabeth saw the defeat of the Spanish Armada as a God approved Protestant victory; and she saw it as proof that God had been on her side during the crisis. Elizabeth's famous speech made at Tilbury to rally men to the cause was in fact made after England was safe from the Catholic enemy and so there was little risk to her person. The famous speech she is said to have delivered is now one of the best known dialogues in history. Elizabeth and her trusted counsellors, Walsingham and Burghley were the original political spin doctors and turned this victory into a Protestant triumph led by their virtuous Protestant Virgin Queen. The legacy are the words she is said to have spoken at Tilsbury:

'My loving people,

We have been persuaded by some that are careful of our safety, to take heed how we commit ourselves to armed multitudes, for fear of treachery; but I assure you I do not desire to live to distrust my faithful and loving people. Let tyrants fear. I have always so behaved myself that, under God, I have placed my chiefest strength and safeguard in the loyal hearts and good-will of my subjects; and therefore I am come amongst you, as you see, at this time, not for my recreation and disport, but being resolved, in the midst and heat of the battle, to live and die amongst you all; to lay down for my God, and for my kingdom, and my people, my honour and my blood, even in the dust.

I know I have the body but of a weak and feeble woman; but I have the heart and stomach of a king, and of a king of England too, and think foul scorn that Parma or Spain, or any prince of Europe, should dare to invade the borders of my realm: to which rather than any dishonour shall grow by me, I myself will take up arms, I myself will be your general, judge, and rewarder of every one of your virtues in the field.

I know already, for your forwardness you have deserved rewards and crowns; and We do assure you in the word of a prince, they shall be duly paid you. In the meantime, my lieutenant general shall be in my stead, than whom never prince commanded a more noble or worthy subject; not doubting but by your obedience to my general, by your concord in the camp, and your valour in the field, we shall shortly have a famous victory over those enemies of my God, of my kingdom, and of my people." *(British Library, Harley 6798, f.87)*

This crisis in Elizabeth's reign is important for many reasons. It muted the cold war between Spain and England, and although Spain did attempt to invade again it was not on the same scale as before. The defeat of the Spanish armanda was also an excellent propaganda opportunity for Burghley and Walsingham. Elizabeth had a portrait of herself with the battle taking place behind her, this picture with its imagery helped to feed into the lasting mythology and imagery of Elizabeth. On a more practical level, the crisis gave Drake and the English navy the opportunity to devise new naval battle stratagems for future use. Lastly, the armada was the start of the decline of Spain, as a superpower. While Spain declined it was also the point that many historians agree was the beginning of the rise of the English navy that would go on to dominate world history for several centuries and help to create the British Empire.

1601: The Essex Rebellion

To understand the motivation behind this particular uprising it is important to look at the man who gave his name to the rebellion, Robert Devereux, 2nd Earl of Essex. Essex was the stepson of the late Robert Dudley, Earl of Leicester. Unlike any other uprising throughout the reign of Elizabeth, this one was not undertaken in the name of God either Catholic or Protestant; it wasn't even a protest against harsh social conditions of the poor. It was instead motivated by one spoilt young man's ego and his immature reaction to losing his position as Elizabeth's favourite. Robert Devereux was a youth who had no natural ability for politics. Due to his status, he had no life skills apart from charming women and fighting. He was emotionally immature and grew to resent how a now aged Elizabeth had spurned him after he had failed in the elevated military position that she had granted to him.

Essex was first presented at court during 1584 by his stepfather, the Earl of Leicester. He soon caught Elizabeth's eye, for she liked to be surrounded by lively, attractive young men in her court. Fifteen months before Leicester's death, Essex succeeded his stepfather in the lucrative and highly sort after role of Master of the Horse. He would go on to inherit all his stepfather's courtly perks after his death in September 1588. Elizabeth may have been a queen, but she was also a woman. Her favouritism towards Essex increased after her beloved Leicester died. In her grief for her beloved friend, who had been the closest thing that the self-styled Virgin Queen had had as a life partner, platonic or otherwise, she seems to have transferred a lot of her affection to his attractive young stepson. She even took to calling Essex 'Robin' as she had done with Dudley. Sadly, this favour only made Essex think that he could behave as he wanted. He came to believe that he was untouchable and was able to talk himself out of any trouble he found himself in by charming Elizabeth.

Being a queen, especially a queen who chose not to share her royal burden with a spouse must have felt very lonely, especially as Elizabeth aged. Many of her loyal advisors, who had been with her for years, were starting to pass away and Elizabeth found comfort and solace in Essex's easy charm and attention. Elizabeth liked the attention so much that she tried to prevent him from taking part in what became known as the English Armada. This English Armada was helping Portugal fight Spain during the spring and early summer of 1589. Even though Elizabeth forbade him from joining Francis Drake and her navy, Essex stole away in the middle of the night to join up and help the English fleet. The whole venture was a very expensive failure. Upon his safe return to court, Elizabeth forgave her favourite for his disobedience which only set a bad precedent and gave him a false sense that he was untouchable.

Elizabeth was not the only woman at court that Essex was charming and wooing. Sir Francis Walshingham's daughter, also named Frances, fell prey to Essex's charm and flattery. The pair eventually married during 1590. It was now that Elizabeth started to suspect the loyalty of her once devoted favourite. As punishment to both Frances and Essex for their happiness, Elizabeth sent Essex to help Henri VI of France against her old enemy, Spain. While helping the French, Essex took part in the capture of Cadiz during the summer of 1596. Questions were later asked about the use of official funds, and in particular what Essex had done with these funds. This caused further distrust towards Elizabeth's former favourite.

Before his mother Lettuce Knowles remarried the Earl of Leicester in late 1565, a young Essex became a ward of court and went to live with the Cecil family at Burghley House. He was the same age as Cecil's own son, Robert Cecil who would follow his father into politics. Robert Cecil suffered with a condition that caused a curvature of the spine, this is known as scoliosis, the same birth defect that Richard III had. The condition caused Robert Cecil to be of short stature and as a consequence he was more scholarly and less sporty than his peer. The young Cecil suffered taunts and bullying from his father's ward, Essex. Consequently, the young men never got along, and their mutual dislike of each other continued when they both rose to Elizabeth's privy council.

By the end of the 1590s, Elizabeth as well as many on her privy council had grown tired of the arrogant, vain popinjay that Essex had become. So, when insurrection threatened in Ireland, then a single country and considered by the English to be under their rule, the council and Elizabeth thought that it was an excellent opportunity for the Earl of Essex to prove himself. Essex became the Lord Lieutenant of Ireland and went over with a sizeable force to put down the unrest. The leader of the Irish insurrection was Hugh O'Neil, Earl of Tyrone. Once again questions were raised about where the money for the campaign went, Essex took it upon himself to bestow honours on his favourites, thinking that this would encourage loyalty, rather than through strong leadership. Instead of crushing Tyrone through military engagement, Essex chased smaller insignificant skirmishes around in the south of Eire and sort a truce with the Earl of Tyrone without consent from either the privy council or Elizabeth. The truce was a step too far as the privy council was concerned, feeling that Essex had shamed England in this course of action.

When news of the truce made its way back to London, Essex was immediately ordered to return home where he was cross-examined by the privy council. The council concluded that his mismanagement and unauthorised surrender to Tyrone was inexcusable and was viewed as the equivalent of committing military desertion. His punishment was to be confined to house arrest. While under house arrest Essex, tried to charm his way out of trouble by writing the following to Elizabeth: *'Hasten paper to that happy presence whence only unhappy I am banished. Kiss that fayre correcting hand which layes new plasters to my lighter hurts butt to my greatest woond applyeth nothig. Say thou cummest from shaming languishing despairing.'* (6 September 1600, Letter Essex - Elizabeth I SP12/275 f.102)

Elizabeth was no longer susceptible to his charm. It was at this point when his charm stopped working that he started harbouring dangerous anger and resentment towards the queen and her council. He also began to resurrect his boyhood grudge towards Robert Cecil publicly, blaming the whole privy council for his own poor decisions and his loss of favour from Elizabeth.

By November, Essex was ordered to return to Ireland. But the now powerful, Robert Cecil felt that Essex had been treated too leniently in the matter of his poor command as Lord Lieutenant of Ireland and Cecil persistently brought up the matter with the privy council and the queen. In June 1600, Essex was forced to face a commission of 18 peers to examine his conduct. Cecil's revenge was that Essex had to be interrogated while on his knees. His peers ruled against Essex and the consequences were that he was stripped of all his political and public offices and was returned to house arrest. This final humiliation, at the hands of his old rival, Cecil, was too much for Essex and it seems he lost all common sense. He now felt that his only option was to raise an armed force of men and go to court and threaten Elizabeth to abandon Cecil and reinstate his public offices. As well as Essex, the other leading figures who got mixed up in his madcap vengeful plans included the Earl of Southampton, Henry Neville, Sir Charles Danviers, Sir Christopher Blount and Sir John Davis.

The whole scheme was poorly planned by the young hotheads and their plans were neither discreet nor realistic. One of the mistakes that gave Essex away was within his correspondence. He bizarrely asked his successor as Lieutenant of Ireland, Lord Montjoy to send over men to help support his rebellious plans. Like father, like son, Cecil knew of this plan and allowed Essex to continue in order to incriminate himself and be charged with treason. He also must have known that Essex had no hope in succeeding in his hair-brain plot and knew that the queen was never in any real danger, it was a calculated risk that worked in Cecil's favour.

Everything came to a head on the morning of 8 February 1601, when the queen authorised a party of men to go to Essex's home and bring him to court. This was neccessary as he had failed to attend a meeting, he had been called to at the privy council the previous day. When the delegation to fetch the obstinate earl was issued with the summons, Essex acted unwisely and took the delegation party from court hostage. He then decided to ride off into London hoping to recruit support to storm the court. London had been put on high alert and the authorities were told that Essex was a wanted traitor. Unfortunately for Essex, there was very little support for him or his cause; the people of Elizabethan London were not interested in the petty rivalry between the queen's counsellors. People became even more weary as word got out that he was a marked man. With no support, the desperate earl thought that his political hostages would be his best weapon, but upon his return to Essex House, he found no hostages and more of the queen's men waiting for him. The game was up and sensibly Essex surrendered.

Essex faced trial within days, and he was unsurprisingly found guilty of high treason. His punishment was to be death by decapitation. He was given the dignity of execution within the Tower of London rather than upon Tower Hill. He climbed the scaffold to face his punishment on 25 February, seventeen days after the stand-off at Essex House. He was the only one of the main rebels to face the axe for their treason, the others were held in the Tower and fined for their involvement. His wife Frances was left a widow with three children. Luckily, she did remarry, this time to Richard Burgh, the Earl of St Albans.

This last episode in Elizabeth's reign, shows that Elizabeth the woman, was just as vulnerable to the charm of men as any other woman. It also shows that she had grown with age. Elizabeth's attitude towards Essex changed when she suspected that he had become untrustworthy and disloyal to her and she acted swiftly. Elizabeth also knew that he was the main perpetrator of this vain rebellion and decided to show mercy by not carry out trials or executions to the misguided youths who became embroiled in his rash schemes. This compassion is something that her father, Henry VIII certainly did not demonstrate later on in his reign. And yet it must have been personally hard for her as she was dealing with her Robin's stepson. It also shows that even until the end of her long reign, Elizabeth had maintained an efficient, loyal and trust worthy group counsellors within her privy council.

1603: The Death of Elizabeth I

In early 1603, Elizabeth was in her seventieth year. As January 1603 started, Elizabeth's royal court made its last move, to her favourite palace at Richmond. Elizabeth had been keeping signs of her age away from her subjects over the last decades of her reign. She had done this by having idealised portraits of herself commissioned and ensuring that she was never seen by anyone but her most intimate circle of ladies, without her extensive make up and elaborately styled wigs.

The queen's dwindling health was given a sudden shock that would send her on the steady decline to her own demise. In February 1603, news reached the court that the queen's confidante, long term friend and lady-in-waiting, Catherine Howard, (nee Carey), Countess of Nottingham, had died. The countess's mother had been Anne Boleyn's sister, Mary. Mary had been Henry VIII's mistress before Anne went on to become his second queen. Rumour around court was that the queen and the countess may have been in fact half-sisters as well as close friends and cousins. The countess had been in Elizabeth's service for forty-five years and the two women had effectively grown up together. The news of the countess's death brought about insomnia and loss of appetite to the queen. As a result, Elizabeth became restless and refused to get into her bed. Her refusal to go to bed was because she feared she would never get out of bed once she got in. Elizabeth's erratic behaviour increased as she entered the last few weeks of her life and reign.

Over the course of the next few weeks, none of her physical symptoms were particularly serious; she is thought to have been suffering from a nasty throat infection but, mentally it looks like the queen had relinquished her will to keep living. She refused treatments from her physicians and instead turned her thoughts to the heavenly realms of God. The lack of sleep and food made it hard for her to leave her private bedchamber even to participate in daily mass. Near the end of her life, she sat on cushions by her door listening to the royal chapel services. It was the Countess of Nottingham's widower, Charles Howard, Earl of Nottingham, that would eventually coax the queen to get into her bed for the last time, on 22 March 1603. As the Tudor period was drawing to a close the whole of her court held their breath wondering if she would finally name her successor.

On 23 March, her privy council held their last meeting within the dying queen's bedchamber, and it is said that during this last gathering, Elizabeth gestured with her hand at the mention of King James VI of Scotland's name. The privy council, in particular Robert Cecil, chose to interpret this as a non-verbal communication from her majesty, to mean that she agreed to James being the heir to her crown and kingdoms.

That evening only those closest to Elizabeth and the Archbishop of Canterbury, John Whitgift were with the dying queen. Elizabeth did not seem to fear dying as she held on to the elderly Archbishop's hand during their prayers together. The Archbishop, who was four years her senior, was kept kneeling by her bedside despite him growing uncomfortable on his old knees – it was a last kind service of devotion to his queen. The Archbishop himself would die less than eleven months later, aged 74.

Elizabeth slipped in and out of consciousness during that night and eventually died peacefully in her sleep sometime between 2.00 am and 3.00 am. After her death, on 24 March 1603, the body of Queen Elizabeth I was placed inside a lead coffin and carried by night in a torchlit barge along the Thames from Richmond Palace to Whitehall. There, the Queen was to lie in state until her state funeral.

The smooth transition of power to James I after the death of Elizabeth did not just happen; it was all due to the hard work of Sir Robert Cecil. Cecil was most definitely his father's son; he had learnt his statecraft from the best, his father, William Cecil, Lord Burghley. In the last decade of Elizabeth's reign, Cecil had been cautious about approaching James, who was then 37, despite fearing that he blamed Cecil's father, for the death of his mother, Mary Queen of Scots. Communication between the pair did not start frequently until after the Essex Rebellion of 1600. This correspondence between Cecil and the Scottish king took place under cover, using code names and trusted couriers, Cecil even went as far as to have a trusted scribe write the letters so that they could not traced back to him through his handwriting. The reason for this precaution was because technically what Cecil and James were doing was treasonous as they were secretly planning for the inevitable event of the ageing queen's death and James' eventual succession to power. What was most dangerous was that Cecil was planning with a man who had not been officially named as Elizabeth's heir, until the queen's last hours.

As part of this preparation for the succession, Cecil masterminded the creation of the Great Council. This council was given constitutional power to essentially be an interim governing committee that would stand in for the monarch in the event of death or serious illness. This council would legally ratify a successor should one not have been named by the queen prior to her death. But even Cecil was unsure what the future may hold, and he put plans in place to cover all outcomes; he even had a contingency plan in place for himself. He had started to buy up land in the country so that if things did not go politically in his favour upon Elizabeth's death, he could retire quietly and comfortably from political life.

On the morning of the 24 March 1603, Robert Cecil's planning began to be implemented. The Great Council confirmed and proclaimed James Stuart, King of the Scots as England's new monarch at 06:00, just three hours after her death. The only part of the process that Robert Cecil did not have total control over was the when and who was to go to Scotland to inform James that he was now officially King of England, as well as Scotland. The late queen's distant cousin, Robert Carey took it upon himself to slip out of the palace and ride hard and fast up to Scotland to in order to tell James the good news. Carey had greedy motivations for undertaking this task, he wanted to establish himself in the new monarch's favour. Astonishingly, it only took Carey only three days riding, helped by having prearranged horses placed along the route to Edinburgh. He reached James's court on the evening of 26 March and his efforts were rewarded when he was made a gentleman of the new king's bedchamber.

Thankfully, the rest of Sir Robert Cecil's plans were successful. The socio-economic climate of spring 1603 was not good for England. The harvests had failed causing grain prices to rise. The gap between rich and poor had grown larger. Things were so bad that in the last decade of Elizabeth's reign, parliament had created Poor Laws in a vain attempt to help the growing number of impoverished English citizens. Inevitably an increase in poverty created steep rise in crime and vagrancy. The golden age of the Tudors had already started to decline in the last decade of Elizabeth's reign.

As well as social and economic upheaval at the time of Elizabeth's death, the court and the public at large worried about succession. One of the biggest fears was whether or not there would be a counter-reformation after Elizabeth's death. This uncertainty stemmed from a fear of an uprising from Catholics that had started to grow since the execution of Mary Queen of Scots and had been further exasperated by the failed attempt to invade England by the Spanish Amanda in 1588. In short, the Anglicans of England, the non-conformist Protestants and the Catholic minority all feared the unknown. Their biggest worry was for the future of their souls and that they might find themselves persecuted for their religious beliefs. Elizabeth had been a moderate Protestant and had not been extreme in her religious convictions, unlike her Protestant brother, King Edward VI or her Catholic sister Queen Mary I.

There was also a small fear amongst those in power at the time of the queen's death that the English people would not accept James as their new king because he was Scottish and therefore the old enemy – however a Scottish King was still preferable to the majority compared to the potential continental candidates.

Uncertainty was also due to the fact that even though king James VI was the most logical heir to Elizabeth's throne, he was not the only possible candidate for the position. There were possible heirs descending from John of Gaunt's second marriage to Constance of Castile; all of whom were foreign and Catholic. The first of these possible contenders was the daughter of Elizabeth's former half-brother-in-law, Philip II. She was the Infanta Isabella Clara Eugenia. Also descended from John of Gaunt was the Duke of Braganza's eldest son, Ranuccio I Farnese, Duke of Palma who was both Catholic and Portuguese. Thankfully for the English Protestants both the Infanta Isabella and Duke of Palma were too busy with their own continental affairs at the time of Elizabeth's death. Circumstances were helped because the pair had no encouragement from King Philip III of Spain. The reason Philip III did not help either a Spanish infanta or a Portuguese duke take the English throne was because this would have upset the new stable status quo between the old rivals of Spain and France.

Closer to home, there was also another potentially troublesome possible claimant; Lady Arabella Stuart. Born in 1575, Arabella Stuart came from an impressive aristocratic bloodline which meant that she was related to both the English and Scottish royal dynasties. Her maternal great-grandmother was Henry VIII's sister, Margret Tudor who had married James IV of Scotland. After the death of her first husband the dowager queen Margret remarried into the Cavendish family. Margaret's daughter was Arabella's grandmother, the formidable and canny Tudor businesswoman, Elizabeth Cavendish who is better known throughout history as Bess of Hardwick. Bess was an extraordinary woman of the sixteenth century; fortune favoured her as she married well four times and ran highly profitable estates from her dowager lands. Arabella's paternal linage is no less impressive as her uncle was the ill-fated second husband of Mary Queen of Scots, Henry Stuart, Lord Darnley, making her cousin to James VI who would go on to inherit the English throne as James I of England.

The main issue against Arabella inheriting the English throne upon the death of Queen Elizabeth, was that the leading politician of Elizabeth's court, Robert Cecil favoured James VI over Arabella. After the reigns of three queens (three if you count Jane Grey's nine-day reign) Cecil felt that England needed the stability of a king rather than a queen. The role of female monarch had proved problematic dynastically for the Tudors as both Elizabeth and Mary had failed to produce heirs. The issue of their marriages had not only been political, but the sisters had also made the matter personal too. Cecil however felt that the stability of England both domestically and internationally required such decisions to be exclusively political.

With a female monarch there was also the added complication of the status of her husband and the question of whether he should be a commoner or royalty. If he was royalty, he would therefore need to be foreign and of equal status to queen. This then brought a different set of political complications of how much say he should have politically in national decisions as well as what his title should be; consort or joint monarch of England. Elizabeth had cleverly avoided this issue by choosing not to marry, but as a consequence, she had no heirs of her own to inherit the throne. Female monarchs were in a precarious situation should they have heirs. Childbirth in the sixteenth century was still a dangerous moment in a woman's life. When looking at these potential complications from Mary and Elizabeth's reigns, it is easy to understand why Cecil favoured James VI of Scotland over Arabella.

On 28 April 1603, after lying in state at Whitehall for over a month, Elizabeth's coffin was carried from Whitehall to Westminster Abbey on a hearse drawn by horses hung with black velvet. The coffin was covered in a rich purple cloth, topped with an effigy of Elizabeth with a sceptre in her hands and a crown on her head. Above the coffin was a canopy supported by six knights, and behind the hearse was the queen's Master of the Horse, leading her palfrey. The chief mourner was the Countess of Northampton who led the party of peers of the realm, all dressed in black. Details of the queen's funeral service do not seem to have survived however records from Westminster Abbey suggest that there would have been music and that it may have been composed by Thomas Morley. According to the abbey's records, the choirs of the abbey and Chapel Royal were present with other musicians at the queen's funeral.

Elizabeth was then buried at Westminster Abbey in the vault of her grandfather, Henry VII, until she was moved in 1606 to her present resting place, a tomb in the Lady Chapel of Westminster Abbey which she shares with her step-sister Mary I. King James I spent over eleven thousand pounds on Elizabeth I's lavish funeral, and he also arranged for this white marble monument to be built. The tomb is inscribed with the words: 'Consorts both in throne and grave, here we rest two sisters, Elizabeth and Mary in hope of our resurrection.'

Conclusion

Throughout this work I have endeavoured to use my knowledge, research skills and experience to try to demonstrate an understanding of the woman, the politician and the queen who was the last Tudor monarch, Queen Elizabeth I.

As we discovered during the first part of the book, Elizabeth had an extraordinary and somewhat disruptive childhood, which was in no way thought of as ordinary, even for a high status young lady from the sixteenth century. Her early life experiences taught the young Elizabeth important lessons about living as part of the Tudor royal family and how not only to survive but to thrive, both as a woman and later as a queen. These experiences would go on to influence the decisions she made as a queen, both politically, religiously, and also the choices she made as a woman.

I believe the biggest influence from her childhood, was living with the notoriety and legacy of her mother; whose death, thankfully, the young Elizabeth had been too young to remember clearly. The experiences and fates of her four stepmothers, Jane Seymour, Anne of Cleves, Catherine Howard and Katherine Parr would have shown her the best ways to survive as a woman in the sixteenth century too.

It wasn't just the women of her childhood who would have influenced Elizabeth, her father Henry VIII, also left a lasting impression on his second daughter. Like him, Elizabeth embraced the power of art. If you were to ask the average person on the street what Henry or Elizabeth looked like, the majority of people would be able to describe a picture of Henry with his legs apart, his prominent codpiece, hands on hips, his beard and hat taken from the iconic Holbein painting. Likewise, when you think of Elizabeth as a queen you think of her ruffs, embroidered gowns, pale face, red hair, pearls and that very upright position she adopted in all of her portraits. This use of art was also exceptionally effective during their lifetimes as well as historical references today.

Conclusion

In an age of low literacy and none of the twenty-first century media outlets, these images of both Henry and later Elizabeth, were visually recognisable to their subjects. This was of course also because both father and daughter undertook visits up and down the country so that their subjects knew what they looked like.

The other big life lesson Elizabeth learnt from her father was surrounding the thorny subject of marriage. Witnessing her father's behaviour as she grew up showed an intelligent young woman that sixteenth century marriage was not equal between the genders. Henry's power and might as king merely exaggerated the inequalities other high-status women of the time dealt with day to day. Many of the problems Mary Queen of Scots had with her second husband, Lord Darnley, came from him wanting to have equality if not total dominance within the relationship. Elizabeth's step-sister Mary I, tried to avoid that issue by marrying a man with equal status - Philip II of Spain. However, this too had its complexities, Philip as a king himself had his own lands to rule, so was away from her frequently. Philip also attempted to legally become Mary's successor in order to gain something from the marriage - when Mary stopped Philip's plans in her last will, he then attempted to get this by asking Elizabeth to marry to his advantage - unsuccessfully. All the women that her father married, with the exception of Anne of Cleves, (who was wise enough to give Henry what he wanted) all came away from their marriages to Henry worse off, and in Anne Boleyn and Catherine Howard's cases they lost their heads and their lives. Elizabeth therefore probably chose to stay single in order to maintain more political power both domestically within her court and internationally by using her persona of the Virgin Queen.

The period of Elizabeth's life between the death of her father in 1547 and the eleven years until she eventually ascended the throne in 1558, were not only hugely suggestible years due to her age but they were also the most dangerous period of her life. During the short Protestant reign of her half-brother, King Edward VI, was the victim of men in power, most notably the man acting as her stepfather, Thomas Seymour, while in the care of her stepmother Katherine Parr. Elizabeth fell prey to him in a place where she should have been protected - her home. Elizabeth's experience with the Seymour scandal, can be clearly reflected in the advice that she gave Mary Queen of Scots in the aftermath of the suspicious death of her second husband. Sadly, Mary failed to take heed of Elizabeth's sage advice.

It was also during this period that Elizabeth met some of her most important advisors and friends, who would serve her well once she ascended the throne. Robert Dudley, Earl of Leicester and William Cecil, Lord Burghley being the two notable advisors and friends the queen kept and trusted throughout her reign. The lessons of her tempestuous childhood and adolescence taught Elizabeth that loyalty was of the utmost importance to her personally and as a queen. Both Burghley and Leicester were two men who could speak truthfully to the queen even if it meant upsetting her.

In the last section of the book I endeavoured to show how circumstances and events within Elizabeth's 45-year reign of England were influenced by her previous life experiences and lessons and how they affected the choices she made and how she handled certain situations.

Some things, such as Elizabeth's wish not to marry she held on to. However, decisions she had to make that were much harder for her usually involved her family. Elizabeth struggled with signing the Duke of Norfolk's death warrant even though he had clearly committed treason. She had the same issue again with her cousin, Mary Queen of Scots. This was further complicated due to Mary's status as an anointed Queen. Elizabeth was initially uncomfortable about meddling with issues of faith and even famously saying she 'did not want to make windows into men's souls' and she claimed that she saw religion as a private and personal matter. It was only after the pope forced her to make it political with the papal bull and excommunication that she reluctantly followed a harder line influenced by advice of Walshingham and Burghley. This issue came to a climax during the attempted invasion of Philip II's Spanish Armada in 1586.

To conclude, Queen Elizabeth I was one of English history's most successful survivors because she learnt from other peoples' mistakes and adapted. This helped her maintain control of her reign. She was careful about the people she chose to be around her, and she was wise enough to learn from the mistakes of others as well as from her own. For a woman, and as an heir who should not have technically ever become queen, Elizabeth did not just succeed where her half-siblings and her cousin Mary Queen of Scots had failed, but her reign has been remembered as The Golden Age. Successful people learn and grow from their past and and strive to avoid making the same mistakes again. Elizabeth I got this down to an art form and for me she is one of our greatest historical figures because of this.

Bibliography

Primary Sources

BURGHLEY, W. Cecil Lord, *A collection of state papers relating to affairs in the reigns of Henry VIII, Edward VI, Mary and Elizabeth 1542-1570.* Transcribed from original letters, edited by Samuel Haynes, W Bowyer, London, 1740.

COVERDALE, Myles (English translator*), The Coverdale Bible,* 1535.

HARLEY, Robert, The Harleian Manuscripts, Rolls at The British Museum.

HARRIS, Carrie, *State trials of Mary Queen of Scots, Sir Walter Raleigh and Captain William Kidd. Condensed and copied from the state trials of Francis Hargrave esq, London,* 1776.

HARRISON, G.B., *The Letters of Queen Elizabeth,* Cassell, 1935.

HARTLEY, T.E. (ed.), *Proceedings of the Parliaments of Elizabeth I,* Volume 1, 1558- 1581.

HAYWARD, Sir John, *Annals of the first four years of the reign of Queen Elizabeth.* Edited from a manuscript in the Harleian collection, by John Bruce, London. Printed for the Camden society, by J. B. Nichols and son, 1840.

HOLINSHED, Raphael, WOLFE, Reyner, STANIHURST, Richard, HARRISON, William, CAMPION, Edmund, *The First Volume of the Chronicles of England, Scotland and Ireland,* 1577, London (BL G.6006-7).

POLLEN, J. Hungerford (ed.) *Mary Queen of Scots & the Babington Plot,* The Scottish History Society, Third Series Vol III, Edinburgh University Press by T&A Constable Ltd. for the Scottish History Society, 1922.

STOWE, John, *The Annales of England,* faithfully collected out of the most authentic authors, records until 1592, London, 1600.

WINGFIELD, Robert, *Account of the Trial, Execution and Burial of Mary Queen of Scots* (MS 81), 1586.

From the British Library Collections

BL 5751A f.87 signet warrant, 19 May 1574
BL Cotton Charter IV
BL Egerton 2806 f.11 warrant, 16 October 1568
BL Egerton 2806 f.135 warrant, 26 September 1578.
BL Egerton 2806 f.152, 12 April 1580
BL Egerton 2806 f.6 14, April 1568.
BL Egerton 2806 f70 warrant, 28 September 1575
BL Egerton 2800 f.20 warrant, 10 April 1579.
BL, Harley 6798 f.87 (Tilbury speech)
BL Stowe MSS555 fo.138
BL MS 48027/FOS 639 (*Account of Mary Queen of Scots Execution*)

From the Calendar of State Papers

Calendar of State Papers (Venetian), 1558-80, page 94, letter dated 30 May 1559, from Il Schifanoya to the Castellan of Mantua.
Calendar of State Papers (Foreign), 1577-78
Calendar of State Papers (Foreign), 1577-78
Calendar of State Papers (Spain), Volume 4 1529-1530
Calendar of State Papers (Spain), Volume 13, 1554-1558
Calendar of State Papers (Spain), Volume 14, 1558-67
Calendar of State Papers (Venetian), 1558-80

Transcripts

Coroner's Report into the death of Amy Robsart, KB9/1073/f.80, National Archives Kew.
Elizabeth's 'Golden Speech' to Parliament, 30 November 1601, ref: SP12/282ff.137r_141v
Elizabeth I's Personas in an Extemporaneous Speech to Parliament, 10 February 1559.
Elizabeth I to Mary Queen of Scots, 24 February 1567, ref: SP52/13f.17, National Archives Kew.

Letters

NLS MS 54.1.1 (The last letter of Mary Queen of Scots).
Robert Devereux, Earl of Essex to Elizabeth I, 6 September 1600 (SP12/275 f.102).
The 'Tide Letter', National Archives, Kew 17 March 1554, (Sp 11/4/2 f.3-3v).

Web Sources

Papal Bull issued against Queen Elizabeth, 27 April 1570, via http://www.papalencyclicals.net/Pius05/p5regnans.htm

Secondary Sources

ADAMS, Simon (ed.), *Household Accounts and Disbursement Books of Robert Dudley, Earl of Leicester*, Volumes 1-6.
ARCHER, J.E., GOLDRING, E., and KNIGHT, S. (ed.), *The Progresses, Pageants and Entertainments of Queen Elizabeth I,* Oxford University Press, Oxford, 2007.
ARNOLD, Janet, *Queen Elizabeth's Wardrobe Unlock'd*, Routledge, 1988.
BINDOFF, S.T., *Tudor England*, Pelican, 1950.
CAMDEN, William, *The history of the most renowned and victorious Princess Elizabeth, late Queen of England*, 1675.
COLE, Mary Hill, *The Portable Queen: Elizabeth I and the Politics of Ceremony*, University of Massachusetts Press, 2011.
COLLINS, Arthur Jefferies, *The Inventory of Jewels and Plate of Queen Elizabeth I of England in 1574,* Trustees of the British Museum, 1955.
CROFT, Pauline, *Patronage, Culture and Power: The Early Cecils 1558-1612*, Yale University Press, 2002.
DUNN, Jane, *Elizabeth and Mary: Cousins, Rivals, Queens*, Harper Collins, 2003.
DURKHEIM, Émile, *The Elementary Forms of Religious Life* (edited by Mark S. Cladis, translated by Carol Cosman), Oxford University Press, Oxford, 2008.

ELTON, Geoffrey Rudolph, *Reform and Reformation, England 1509-1558*, Edward Arnold Ltd, 1977.

GUY, John, *Elizabeth the Forgotten Years*, Viking, 2016.

GUY, John, *My Heart Is My Own: The Life of Mary Queen of Scots*, Fourth Estate, 2004.

HAIGH, C., (editor) *The Reign of Elizabeth I*, Palgrave, 1984.

HALL, Edward, *Halls Chronicle: Containing the History of England During the Reign of Henry IV and the succeeding Monarchs to the end of the reign of Henry VIII, in which are particularly described the manners and the customs of those periods*, Forgotten books, April 2018.

HUTCHINSON, Robert, *The Spanish Armanda*, Thomas Dunne Books, 2014.

JENKINS, Elizabeth, *Elizabeth the Great*, Phoenix, 1958.

LEVINE, Mortimer, *Tudor Dynastic Problems 1460-1571*, (edited by G R Elton), George Allen & Unwin Ltd, 1973.

MACNALTY, Sir Arthur S., *Mary Queen of Scots: Daughter of Debate*, Christopher Johnson Publications, London, 1960.

MAUSS, Marcel, *The Gift: Forms and Functions of Exchange in Archaic Societies*, 1924.

NICHOLS, J.G., (editor) *Literary Remains of King Edward the Sixth*, Vol II, London, J. B. Nichols and Sons for the Roxburghe Club, 1857.

NICHOLS. John, *Progresses and public processions of Queen Elizabeth,* Volume I, 1823.

NICHOLS. John, *Progresses and public processions of Queen Elizabeth,* Volume II, 1823.

NICHOLS. John, *Progresses and public processions of Queen Elizabeth,* Volume III, 1823.

PARKER, Geoffrey, *Europe in Crisis: 1598-1648*, Fontana paperbacks, 1979.

PLOWDEN, Alison, *Danger to Elizabeth: The Catholics Under Elizabeth* I, The History Press, 2011.

PLOWDEN, Alison, *Elizabeth Regina*, The History Press, 2011.

PLOWDEN, Alison, *Marriage With My Kingdom: The Courtships of Elizabeth I*, The History Press, 2011.

PLOWDEN, Alison, *Two Queens in One Isle: The Deadly Relationship of Elizabeth I and Mary Queen of Scots*, The History Press, 2004.

PLOWDEN, Alison, *The Young Elizabeth*, The History Press, 2011.

PORTER, Linda, *Katherine the Queen: The Remarkable Life of Katherine Parr*, Picador, 2010.

SKIDMORE, Chris, *Death and the Virgin: Elizabeth, Dudley and the Mysterious Fate of Amy Robsart*, Orion, 2010.

SKIDMORE, Chris, *Edward VI, The Lost King of England*, W&N, 2007.

SOMERSET, Lady Anne, *Elizabeth I*, W&N, 1999.

STARKEY, David, *Elizabeth: Apprenticeship*, Vintage, 2001.

STONE, J.M., *Mary I: Queen of England*, Sands & Co., 1901.

STRICKLAND, Agnes, *Lives of the Queens of England*, 1840-8.

WEIR, Alison, *Mary Queen of Scots and the Murder of Lord Darnley*, Pimlico, 2003.

Index